carefree GOLF

carefree GOLF

LAURA DAVIES

with Lewine Mair

Hodder and Stoughton
London Sydney Auckland Toronto

British Library Cataloguing in Publication data
is available from the British Library

ISBN 0-340-50845 0

First published in Great Britain 1991

Published by Hodder and Stoughton,
a division of Hodder and Stoughton Ltd,
Mill Road, Dunton Green, Sevenoaks, Kent TN13 2YA
Editorial Office: 47 Bedford Square, London WC1B 3DP

Designed by Trevor Spooner

Photoset by SX Composing Ltd, Rayleigh, Essex

Printed in Great Britain by Butler & Tanner Ltd, Frome and London

To my family, whose support has
had most to do with such success
as I have had.

CONTENTS

INTRODUCTION

"When I look at top players such as Bernhard Langer and Seve Ballesteros, I am trying, first and foremost, to pick up their rhythm. Having watched them hit a few shots, I play those shots over and over again in my head, almost as I would a song. Then, when I go to the practice ground, all I am trying to do is to reproduce that timing and feel."

Golf has come easily to Laura Davies who, after winning the British Women's Open of 1986, captured the following year's American Women's Open title at what was only her second attempt.

In this book, she is anxious that her 'simple' approach should come across, for she is convinced that there are golfers everywhere who would play better if they shrugged off some of the often con-flicting theories they have taken on board over the years.

Laura Davies is not the first successful woman golfer to have learned by imitation. Although she is far too unassuming to feel comfortable with having her name linked with that of Lady Heathcoat-Amory, née Joyce Wethered, the early years of these two great Surrey golfers have much in common. They both started out from playing with an older brother. Joyce Wethered and her brother, Roger, who was to lose out to Jock Hutchinson in a play-off for the 1921 Open, would together keep 'temperature charts' of their daily scores on the walls of their holiday home in Dornoch. Miss Wethered later played with her brother's friends at Oxford and she remembers many more matches with them than with her contemporaries in the women's game.

It was this background which led to Miss Wethered winning three British championships and five successive English titles before touring America as a professional – a tour in which she made some £4,000 through playing fifty-two exhibition matches with the top American professionals and amateurs of the day.

Playing from a bunker in 1989.

Laura's brother, Tony, played with his younger sister every night after school and during school holidays. As teenagers they practised side by side, played matches and, of course, tried to out-hit each other. Now that Tony carries Laura's clubs around the golfing globe, they are obviously benefiting from the intimacy and shared knowledge developed over those years.

Lady Amory has memories of one formal lesson but basically she learned, like Laura, by copying others. Her father often took her and Roger to see players like Vardon and Taylor in action and later she was tremendously influenced by Bobby Jones.

"After watching Bobby Jones, I made my backswing longer and endeavoured to have the club pointing to the hole at the top. My swing probably never did look like his – but I liked to think that it did."

Laura, for her part, began by watching her heroes on television. Her iron play is based on Bernhard Langer's: "He has this lovely rhythm I like to copy . . ."

Seve Ballesteros has been the inspiration for her short game, with Laura giving the impression that she is on the Spaniard's wavelength when it comes to seeing and feeling the little shots around the green.

It is an impression endorsed by Amy Alcott, one of the most celebrated professionals on the L.P.G.A. circuit. "Some people," said Amy, "have a touch of magic in their hands. It is what makes them artists, not just golfers. It is not just mechanics, it's more than that. Laura has that magic."

In terms of on-course approach, Lady Amory and Laura do not come into the same category. Where Lady Amory had the ability to wrap herself 'in a cocoon of concentration' for an entire match, Laura confesses cheerfully to being able to concentrate only for as long as she is standing over the ball. But neither of these two great champions has ever wavered from the view that golf should be fun rather than all-consuming and that, in the last resort, it is only a game. Lady Amory always liked to dabble in tennis and fishing, while Laura is apt to punctuate every tournament with some kind of leisure activity. Even during so major an event as the 1990 L.P.G.A. championship, she spent her evenings playing tennis.

At a time when many of the girl professionals, with so much at stake financially, tend to be compared to robots, Laura's carefree approach is wonderfully refreshing. She says that if the money were suddenly to drop out of the professional scene, she would simply take aim once more on the Surrey Ladies' amateur side.

For Laura, golf has never been a matter of hitting one carefully contrived shot after another. She would like others to share in the excitement of giving the ball an uninhibited blow, for she has watched countless golfers – particularly women – who have never come close to hitting the ball hard: "They have these lovely set-ups and backswings but are apt to ruin everything by decelerating into impact."

It could be fear of losing a ball; it could be that they are too pre-occupied with doing what is right: either way, Laura hopes in these pages to contribute to a reduction rather than a multiplication of her readers' golfing worries.

Lewine Mair

EARLY YEARS

One of the great joys of golf lies in the fact that it is a game you can play on your own.

In my later teens, I would spend day after day on the practice ground at West Byfleet. My mother, Rita, would drop me off on her way to work and pick me up at six o'clock on her way home. And in all those hours the only time I would take off would be a mid-day spell in which I would stay in the clubhouse for just as long as it took me to feed my lunch money into the fruit machine.

I never had any lessons but, by the time I started at fourteen, my brother Tony was already pretty keen and was in a position to show me roughly what to do. I have always enjoyed sport on television and I had watched a lot of golf and could not wait to try to imitate men like Jack Nicklaus, Tom Watson and Seve Ballesteros.

During the school holidays, when Tony was at work, I would put in hours and hours of practice. I would think up a shot and then try fifty of them.

LEARNING BY FEEL

I learned by feel how to hook and slice. A lot of people have suggested that my golf is of the 'hit and hope' variety, but the fact is that early on I instinctively understood very much more about my own swing than the girl who takes lessons and accepts everything her professional tells her to do, without considering the advice at all.

Lessons would have been a wicked waste of money for me because in my teenage years I was not prepared to listen to anyone concerning the way the game should be played. I always used to think that I knew best and remember how, when I went to England training sessions with Vivien Saunders, a former British Open champion who has had great success with many of her pupils, she and I would do nothing but argue. For instance, she

worried that I was standing too far from the ball and stretching. The stretching may account for my slight sway, but I have always played like that and by the time Vivien got to me that sway was firmly entrenched in my swing.

With Tony, my brother and first golfing partner.

That I am my own teacher has helped enormously on a professional scene where most players feel completely lost if something goes wrong with their technique. For example, when you are on tour in a country like the United States, you cannot always fly home to your professional, even if he is based somewhere in-America. And he is unlikely to be able to fly out to you, although there have been cases where a group of players have got together and paid for a professional to make a fortnightly visit to the circuit.

Although I was uncooperative at national training, I did value the tips I used to get from Peter Cheal at West Byfleet. He would never stand over me while I was practising but he would often come across and play a shot for me once or twice and I would then copy him.

Dave Regan, the current professional at West Byfleet, followed suit. "The best lesson I can give you," he once said, "is to tell you never to have a lesson. There are certain things built into your swing which may not be right – but they are right for your swing as it is now."

JUNIOR GOLF

At the same time as I was doing all my early practice, I would often join up with the lady members of West Byfleet in the afternoons. I had a great time playing with them. The fact that you are not, as in junior tennis, always fighting it out with someone in your own age group is one of the best things about the game: you are often mixing with an older generation and you learn very quickly to fit in with any age group.

I have fond memories of marathon games with Joy Baker. She would pick me up from the house at about ten to eight in the morning and we would play thirty-six holes, interrupted only by a sandwich lunch. She always set her oven to come on during the afternoon stint and we would return to her house for a slap-up dinner, then she would run me home.

On Friday evenings, I used to play with Howel and Madeleine Thomas. Howel died four years ago but I shall never forget the fun of our regular matches. Thinking about those games today makes me wonder if today's up-and-coming youngsters get as much as they should out of club golf. In their bid to make teams and turn professional, they will often dismiss social golf as a waste of time. In fact, it is the perfect platform for teaching you how to play the game and stay 'loose' at the same time.

Mark Crabtree, Tim Liddington, Joe Maranus and Des Donovan were four more of my old rivals but I must confess that all of these friends saw a rather different Laura to the one who would get so heated in sister versus brother matches.

Opposite:
With Lotta Neumann,
an early opponent in
the European Junior
Team championships.

Tony and I hated to lose to each other. Out of sight of the members, we would chuck clubs, argue with each other and generally behave as you never could if you were playing with anyone else.

I used to delight in club competitions and tournaments like the Hicks Trophy. And I loved playing for a Surrey side in which Jill Thornhill, the 1983 British Champion and one of the most 'professional' amateurs in the game, was almost like a mother figure.

She would tell me off for hitting the wrong shots, wearing the wrong clothes and generally mucking about. But it was because of the Jill Thornhills of this world that I was able to make progress. Much of Jill's experience rubbed off and she was invaluable in helping me to feel at home in the international arena.

JUNIOR INTERNATIONALS

The international occasion I enjoyed the most was the first of my two appearances – in Holland in 1983 – in the European Junior Team championships. I made friends I have to this day and there is a picture hanging on my dining-room wall of me shaking hands with Lotta Neumann at the end of the singles match we played when England, who went on to win the championship, met Sweden. I had the edge that day, winning by two holes, but as I look at the picture, cannot but wonder what odds you could have got against the two of us going on to win the U.S. Women's Open

in successive years.

Although that week was special, there has been nothing to compare with the moment in the 1984 Curtis Cup at Muirfield when I holed downhill from ten feet on the last green to defeat that insatiable golfer Anne Sander. To this day, I can still hear the claps and congratulations from the rest of the Great Britain and Ireland side ringing in my ears as I walked from a hole which, along with Wentworth's seventeenth and eighteenth, ranks as my favourite in all Britain.

TEAM SPORTS

I was brought up on team sport. My uncle talks of how, in childhood years spent in the States when my father, Dave, got a job over there, I was a useful little footballer. At the age of five or six, I would insist on playing alongside the older boys he used to teach.

The team sports I remember playing most vividly are the netball, hockey, tennis and rounders I would play at Fullbrook, the

Weybridge school I attended shortly after returning to England with my mother and brother following the break-up of my parents' marriage. The break-up was difficult at the time but ultimately led to an entirely amicable situation, and the spin-off could not be better for someone in my position.

Many professionals who leave home to play in the States say that the worst part is being so far away from family and friends. That does not apply for me because I have family on both sides of the Atlantic and I am also lucky enough to enjoy a great relationship with my stepfather, 'Uncle Mike'.

I never did any work in the classroom at Fullbrook and this was reflected in my exam results: I took five or six O-Levels and failed the lot. But no-one ever put more effort into school sports. I represented the school at every level at just about every sport although to my eternal disappointment I was never given my colours in any of them.

Though women professionals now have the Solheim Cup, a biennial match against the Americans, I still miss that string of team events which played so important a part in my school and amateur golfing days. But professional golf has its compensations, not the least of which is the travel. Every hole of every course is different, with the game making different demands in different lands.

AROUND THE WORLD

In America, you need to be strong in all departments, while it is no good setting foot in Japan unless you are a genius with the long irons. The courses there are beautifully groomed but they can be a little fiddly, so that you almost feel claustrophobic. I have a set of Japanese clubs made by Maruman and, although I love the driver dearly, it rarely gets the chance to show what it can do in its native land.

The galleries, too, react differently around the world. Where in Britain they would observe a respectful silence for the player who has run up a seven or eight, in Japan the spectators laugh and the player in question laughs with them. The tone of their laughter is sympathetic, suggesting "How absurd it is that this could have happened".

Opposite:
I still miss that string of team events which played so important a part of my school days.

The Japanese are crazy about golf. I have never known a bigger crowd than that which followed Ayako Okamoto and myself as we played together one day in the Konica Open. And when Ayako was involved, along with myself and JoAnne Carner, in the play-off for the 1987 U.S. Open, the live coverage being beamed back to Japan apparently drew the second largest television audience for any golf tournament anywhere in the world – and that includes the men's British Open.

Japanese and British spectators are very knowledgeable but if you want to be inspired you should play in front of an American audience.

17

The shot I knocked onto the green at the 493 yards, uphill seventeenth in the play-off for the 1987 U.S. Open at Plainfield detonated two hundred and eighty yards of applause. It started at the green as the ball came down and spread right back over the hill to where I was standing.

The Swedes are a bit flat as golf watchers while, in France and Italy, I find myself watching the galleries rather than vice versa. They dress so expensively and well that sometimes it feels as if the people on the other side of the ropes are on couturiers' catwalks.

THE ROLE OF PRACTICE ON TOUR

I love the bustle of professional tournaments but, as I found in the three weeks I spent on my own during my first trip to Japan, professional golf can, if you let it, be a bitterly lonely way of life. That is not for me. In contrast to those solitary vigils I used to keep on the practice ground, I now like to be constantly in the company of friends, having fun. You would never, for example, find me doing what Kitrina Douglas does, coming in through the dusk from the practice ground long after everyone else is sitting down to dinner, but I do admire her greatly for her application and for the way in which she is always 100 per cent prepared for a tournament.

Apart from not wanting to practise in isolation, I would never go out and play holes on my own. It is years since I have done that. In order to concentrate, I nowadays need someone to play with and something riding on the day's play. A practice round can be completely wasted as far as I am concerned if I am not playing for £10 a corner or lunch – I need the motivation of the bet to make me think.

All my practice shots are hit before I go out on the course and it is only if I am doing something very wrong that I venture out at the end of a round. The American professionals automatically go out for a good hour after a round, as do many of the girls on the European tour. But when, like me, you are playing as many as thirty-seven tournaments per year, it seems silly to beat too many balls.

If you do anything to excess it becomes boring – as I found out to my cost in the 1988 Nestlé World Championships in the States. I was over there for just one week and, with the travel and the amount of play I had had in the preceding weeks, I was walking the fairways but feeling nothing. However hard I tried, I could not make myself care how I was playing.

Most of the time I am wide awake and relishing not just the golf but also my surroundings. There are some professionals so uptight about their games that they see little beyond the confines of their own swings. They never, to borrow from Walter Hagen, "stop to smell the flowers along the way".

As much as any of the great golfing moments I have enjoyed, there are spectacular pictures which will stay with me all my days.

Pictures of such as the school of whales which frolicked off the coast adjacent to Princeville's seventh fairway as I was playing in Hawaii's Kempa Open; and of a snow-capped Mount Fuji. The mountain provides an awesome backcloth to the sixth fairway in the Konica event.

Many people travel simply to see these things – and the fact that I am seeing them in the course of my work gives me quite a kick. And if ever I need reminding of my good fortune, I only have to think about motor-racing's Nigel Mansell, my partner in a recent *pro-am* tournament. When I see how much golf means to someone who has the resources to fly planes, race yachts and ski in the most exclusive of resorts, I know that I have chosen well.

GETTING STARTED

LEARNING BY IMITATION

If someone gave me a ten-year-old boy to teach, I would buy him a video of his favourite player in action and tell the lad to copy what he saw.

I am not against lesson-taking but I do firmly believe that there can be an alternative.

Lessons are obviously of great value to a receptive child, but it is my conviction that they must be combined with long periods on the practice ground. The pupil must do more than simply repeat what the professional has advised. Only by experimenting with every kind of shot can a golfer develop a real affinity with his clubs.

EQUIPMENT

It is vital that the beginner has equipment which will make the game easier rather than the reverse. All too often you see children and their mothers making do with old clubs which once belonged to the man of the house.

Suitable second-hand clubs can be purchased reasonably cheaply and it makes sense to buy them from a golf professional who has the eye and the knowledge to gauge what is best for his customer.

I learned to play with half a set as a child. But I do not entirely believe that starting with just a few clubs gives you a headstart over the youngster who is given a full set. The usual argument is that the youngster with fewer clubs is going to learn more about improvisation. It is true that Seve Ballesteros started out with just a battered three iron and the young Nancy Lopez had nothing other than a four wood as she followed in the wake of her parents' games but there are plenty of top Americans who have started out with virtually the full complement – and who have still learned to be adaptable. After all, there are always going to be occasions when a shot was asking to be hit low or round branches.

20

ADVICE

If bad equipment can hold a player back, so too can the diverse snippets of information from golf's self-appointed experts.

I believe that aspiring golfers should try, in the politest possible way, to keep their ears blocked, in the politest possible way, for I can think of case after case where players have taken so much advice from so many different sources that their swings have become piecemeal affairs. This, incidentally, has happened to some of the best-known names in their desperation to recapture form.

THE GRIP

It is probably as well for the player who has elected to learn by imitation to have a professional eye cast on his grip from time to time. It is all too easy for the young player trying to belt the cover off the ball to develop 'too strong' a hold on the club, a tell-tale sign being the number of knuckles showing on the left hand. More than three knuckles and the child in question could have his enthusiasm sorely tested by the most vicious of hooks.

The grip must be an amalgam of what is comfortable and correct. I used to have a two-handed hold on the club but the moment I turned professional, I switched to the Vardon or overlapping grip. The only reason I did so was because I fancied a change.

I finished second behind Jan Stephenson in my second professional tournament, but I cannot claim that that was because of the

The Vardon, or overlapping, grip.

21

The grip must be an amalgam of what is comfortable and correct.

change of grip. In truth, I can happily play either way, although I do not think I could cope with an interlocking grip. I sense that that would feel restricting.

My grip today feels entirely comfortable and never gives me any problems. However, there are those who point to the 'V' formed between the thumb and index finger of my right hand and tell me it is all wrong. Apparently, it should be pointing in the direction of my right shoulder but it in fact points towards my chin. In other words, my right hand is a little far over as far as the purists are concerned, although I am happy in the belief that it is this right-hand position which contributes to the slight fade I like to get on the ball.

DOWN THE SHAFT

The other aspect of my grip which from time to time has been something of a talking point is the way in which I go down the shaft. Phil Tresidder wrote of it: "Laura's grip is startling to the connoisseur, with some six inches or more at the top of the stick clearly visible while her hands choke down so that the bottom fingers are almost on the metal. The driver seems a mere match-stick in her hands" (*Golf Digest – May 1988*). The habit is one which began in my second year as a professional when I was looking for extra control with the long irons. It then crept into all my other shots and the situation today is that the greater the pressure, the farther I go down the shaft.

Dave Marr seemed a little bemused by this idiosyncrasy when he was commentating on television during the 1987 U.S. Open, but he did say that if Ray Floyd could get away with it, then so could I. He pointed out that it might spell the difference, for some golfers, between hitting a long ball and one that was not quite long enough but added, reassuringly, that a few extra yards in my case were not especially necessary.

It could well be that this is something I might alter in the years to come but, as Lee Trevino once said to Nancy Lopez, "For as long as your swing works, keep it as it is. The time to change is when it stops working."

Where does all this leave beginners? I think they should take aim on the Vardon grip, but not so rigidly that they forget considerations of comfort. In the matter of where to hold the club, begin with the left hand just far enough down the shaft to have the feeling that hand and club would not come adrift were you to swing the club back a little way with the left arm alone.

I would not recommend the novice to copy my penchant for going right down the shaft, but it is something the better player might like to try when he or she loses control.

ALIGNMENT

Once in possession of a sound grip, the player must work, from the outset, on making sure that he always lines himself up on target. Failing to do this will mean that even the best of swings will suffer because the body has to compensate too much if the shot is to fly straight.

The best way of ensuring that you are correctly aligned at the address is to stand behind the area from which you will be hitting and lay down a club along your intended line. Even the advanced player can benefit from this particular discipline. Practice shots dispatched aimlessly will do little to sharpen the game.

PICTURING THE SWING

I cannot stress too much that the swing I use myself – and the one I recommend – does not operate on a series of potted instructions. Instead of having instructions ringing in my ears I see pictures in my mind: pictures which have been built up and constantly refurbished through following golf on television and by visiting major tournaments.

I hope that the reader will find the swing sequences in this book helpful, but the player who is really serious about fulfilling golfing potential should never waste an opportunity to head for a tournament practice ground where he can watch the experts in action and take in the *sound* of a well-struck ball.

RHYTHM

I am not suggesting that you study such complex things as where their clubs are pointing at the top of the backswing or to what extent their wrists are cocking, although there are some golfers who obviously thrive on getting to grips with such things. When I go and look at players like Bernhard Langer or Seve Ballesteros, I am trying, first and foremost, to pick up their rhythm.

Having watched them hit a few shots, I play those shots over and over again in my head, almost as I would a song. Then, when I go to the practice ground all I am trying to do is to reproduce that timing and feel.

One of my favourite tricks, when I have a pressure shot to play, is to pretend I am Langer or Ballesteros. It is a trick I played to particularly telling effect during the 1988 James Capel Guernsey Open, a favourite tournament of mine but one which, alas, has disappeared from the calendar. On the first day, I had to follow Corinne Dibnah and Karen Lunn, my two Australian friends, after the two of them had hit a couple of close-to-perfect shots on to the twelfth green. Casting aside my less than positive thoughts, I put the shot, as it were, 'into Langer's hands'. I used his rhythm and what felt like his swing. I think I can safely say he would have been happy enough with the result, for the shot was actually better than the two that had gone before.

TOUCH

Early learners who find themselves short of 'touch' near the green should try studying Seve as he prepares to pitch or chip. You do not see him placing his hands firmly on his wedge and chipping the ball straightaway. He is constantly adjusting his grip, handling the club almost as if it were alive. Although the Spaniard hits shots I can only dream about, I do think that I feel the same 'vibes' as he does when I have a touch shot to play.

Even if I am naturally gifted in this area, I know that these natural skills have been greatly honed through watching Seve in action. Everyone who studies him should see the experience as a golfing tonic, for no-one, in recent years, has done more than Seve to reintroduce freedom and flair to a game where so many suffer from 'paralysis by analysis'.

PRESSURE

Before starting to talk about pressure, I have a confession to make. **KILLER-INSTINCT**
I have no killer instinct in a match-play situation. In my years as
an amateur, I never went beyond the quarter-finals of the Surrey
championship, nor did I win any of the major match-play titles.

I am, however, in my element against an entire field as opposed
to just one opponent and I can happily handle a play-off situation
because I still feel as if I am trying to come out on top of the pack.

This was the sensation I had when I was playing at Plainfield in
the three-way play-off with JoAnne Carner and Ayako Okamoto
for the 1987 U.S. Open championship. I have never felt as much
pressure as when I mounted the 18th tee with a two-shot lead. It
was incredibly demanding to have to hit that relatively narrow,
tree-lined fairway in such circumstances but it was the kind of
pressure in which I revel.

On those occasions on the course when I do get uptight, and I can **RELAXING ON**
honestly say that they are not all that frequent, my brother Tony **COURSE**
will talk to me about something other than golf: something which
will take my mind off the situation.

During the fourth round at Plainfield, for example, there was a
great deal of tension in the air when we were playing the seventh
hole, a long par five where I had come close to hitting out of
bounds in practice. The way in which Tony and I relaxed at that
point was hardly something we had picked up from such as Jack
Nicklaus or Tom Watson. The two of us sang, although I cannot
quite remember what song. We were miles away from the spectator ropes at the time and you can rest assured that no-one could
have heard us.

But, even if they had, they would not have shaken their heads in
greater disbelief than did JoAnne Carner at what I did at the
penultimate hole in the 1987 U.S. Open play-off.

Considering a shot at the Gothenburg Ladies Open in 1988.

The seventeenth at Plainfield is a long par five: 493 yards to be precise. The hill rises steeply from the tee and leaves you with a second from an uphill lie and no view of the green. Though there were club members who swore that it could not be done by a woman, I had caught the green twice in the first three days and was determined to do so again, despite the fact that I was two shots ahead of Okamoto and three ahead of Carner at the time and that the two of them had already played safe with their seconds.

I unleashed a three wood, against a background of excited whispers – a particularly risky shot from where I was because the ball might well have been killed by the brow of the hill.

To my great glee, I caught the green and having done so looked up to see JoAnne's perplexed smile.

"Why?" she asked, simply.

"No brains," I suggested.

THE THRILL OF PRESSURE

Pressure, to me, is a feeling of excitement rather than nerves. When, for example, I found myself playing with Nancy Lopez on the last day of the 1988 Jamie Farr Toledo Classic, I was itching to show her that I could play a bit. The last thing I wanted was to shoot a 76 or a 77 in her company. In the event, I not only rose to the occasion but found inspiration in it, beating by three shots the player who has long been one of my great heroines.

Some people claim that my bouts of 'rushing' start when I am under pressure. That is not necessarily the case. There are days when it takes nothing more than a thinned bunker shot and subsequent bogey to precipitate a 'rushing' fit. If I get a birdie at the next hole I settle down again but if I drop more shots I start playing quicker and quicker.

Deep down, I feel that I am making a fast getaway from trouble and it is because of the number of times that this fast getaway has been effective that I persist with the habit. Most notably, it worked in the 1988 British Women's Open at Lindrick where I was five over par after seven holes and yet contrived to hand in a two under par 70.

I am most vulnerable, emotionally, when I am having to make a cut in the States. In Britain, the better players do not have this pressure because two 77s will usually be good enough to make the cut. In America it is altogether different. Of the one hundred and forty-four players in a tournament, it is not exaggerating to say that there are sixty possible winners. Two 74s might not take you into the last two days.

There is a lot of fun in the pressure involved in having to get a four at the last hole to win because the alternatives at that point are not all that disastrous. If you drop a couple of shots and finish second or third, all the players, if not the public, will still compliment you on a good week's work. But it is totally different when you need that four to make the cut. There is no pleasure in that pressure.

If you miss the cut, and I have missed several in the States, there is nothing you can say to console yourself. You are simply off down the road to the next tournament. There have been times when I have waited at the scoreboard for four hours and more, hoping that the scoring will rise and that I will suddenly find myself in among the qualifiers. When the moment comes when I must accept that I have failed, I have known myself to feel almost physically sick, on the verge of tears. If anyone comes up to me and asks any kind of question, I have real difficulty in speaking.

CONTROLLING THE PRESSURE

On the whole, the L.P.G.A. professionals tackle pressure well. Many of them have learned about the psychological side of golf at college and, even if they do feel the strain, they know not to let it show. I have shared several pressure situations with South Africa's Sally Little and she has never once given the slightest hint as to how she is feeling.

In contrast, there are still girls on the European tour whose tension is there for all to see. I have also known club golfers who talk themselves into being nervous wrecks. The golfer who is playing for fun should *never* allow the game to grab him in this way. After all, it is not his livelihood and, just as I never feel pressure when I am out ten-pin bowling or playing snooker, so he should recognise that he is out there to relax and to enjoy himself.

This attitude may not come easily but it is well worth acquiring. I have talked of how Tony and I sang to dispel the tension at a crucial point in the U.S. Open, and I have said how, when I have a big shot to play, I will try for a facsimile of someone else's rhythm and timing. I am not the first to admit to such a combination. Pam Barton, the much-feted English golfer who held the American and British titles of 1936, seemed to work along much the same lines. In *A Stroke a Hole*, she talked her readers through a hypothetical round of match-play. Miss Barton has herself at all-square mounting the eighteenth tee:

"It is as well to remember," she wrote, "that in circumstances such as these, the muscles of the body tend to lose their slackness. This will not do. A keyed-up mind is a good thing, but no good can come of tense legs, arms and shoulders. I shall guard against un-natural rigidity in this way. First of all, I shall fix firmly in my mind the image of some perfect swing, like that, say, of Archie Compston or Henry Cotton. Whoever the swing belongs to its main characteristics will be power, rhythm and balance. And once I can visualise it clearly, I shall try and model my own swing on it exactly. Secondly, I may start humming. This will probably startle you. The tune will not be the first thing that comes into my head. Probably it will be a waltz, lilting and rhythmic . . . The idea sounds absurd until you try it out."

Miss Barton went on to say that humming and singing had always been useful to her in golf: "Either, I find, has an excellent effect on over-excitement as well as taut muscles."

Another obvious way to keep 'on-course-pressure' to a mini-mum is to arrive at the club in a leisurely as opposed to a frenetic fashion. Belle Robertson, who played in the Curtis Cups on either side of the match I played at Muirfield in 1984, would never go to the hairdresser's or, say, to the butcher's before a round of golf because either exercise might take longer than she had anti-cipated and she would then find herself rushing to make her start-ing time. Belle got into the habit of leaving everything like this until after she had played.

PREPARATION WITHOUT PRESSURE

You must give yourself every conceivable chance of getting a good shot away off the first tee. Hit a good one and it can set you up for the round. If, on the other hand, you have to trudge off into the woods to find your ball, it puts you in entirely the wrong mood.

Providing I am in the right mood, for I am not one of those to stick rigidly to what I should do when I am not feeling like it, I will go to the practice ground an hour before my tee-off time and aim to hit something in the region of a hundred balls in the space of twenty minutes.

From the practice ground I switch to the practice putting green. Unlike many of my sister professionals, I do not go straight from the practice putting green to the first tee. Instead, I leave myself half an hour to get organised and to check that I have everything I am likely to need.

I have said how lucky I am never to reach the point where I quake with nerves, but the long wait you get on a first tee is something I do not like, not least because of the importance of that first shot. Instead of trying to avoid the pressure by arriving only at the last second, I will be there in good time and spend my last few minutes making sure that I am sufficiently loose to strike the ball. I have always found that the best way of doing this is to have a few really hard swings with a two iron, swishing the club backwards and forwards as opposed to taking one swing at a time.

CONCENTRATING IN BURSTS

I am lucky in that where, for others, pressure can be a cumulative affair, I have always been able to switch off between shots.

Unlike those players who, an hour or so before they start, disappear into their own little world and a concentration process designed to see them through eighteen holes, I concentrate only in bursts. This can help in tournaments where, as happened in the 1990 U.S. Open, there are constant interruptions for thunder and lightning, with players being ferried to and from the course.

I concentrate when I must decide what to do with a shot and

then, after a host of unconnected thoughts have flickered through my head, I concentrate again when I am over the ball.

If I made a deliberate effort to concentrate flat-out from the start of the round, I doubt if I could go three paces before feeling the need to talk to someone.

I can also switch off between rounds and between tournaments. I might talk about a round at night but it would be relaxed chatter rather than the reliving of bad moments out on the course. If I have done something stupid towards the end of a round I tend to be angry for about ten minutes or so when I come in off the course. After that, I forget all about it, telling myself, "What's done is done."

There are better players than I who react in precisely the same way. Curtis Strange is one example. When, during the 1989 British Open at Troon, the tabloids were making out that he was bad-tempered and difficult, those American golf writers who knew him well sprang to his defence, saying how there were never any problems if they gave him a few minutes' breathing space after, say, he had finished with a six.

POSITIVE THINKING

My mother can remember only one occasion when I was still dwelling on a bad round when I got home. That was when I lost six and five to that fine technician, Jane Forrest, in the third round of the European tour's match-play championship. Apparently I arrived back at the house swearing that that was the end of my career. That is the kind of silly thing I will often say before making a more balanced appraisal of the situation.

Some people say that I never admit to playing badly and they are probably right. In the pressroom, if I am being asked to explain a 78 or a 79, I am more likely to put the score down to a couple of bad or unlucky holes than to the fact that my game had crumbled.

If you start talking about playing badly, you talk yourself into more bad play. In fact my biggest mistake, psychologically speaking, was one of complaining, in 1988 and again in 1990, that I was putting badly. What I should have been saying – and what the club golfer should be saying to his or her inquisitors in such a situation – is, "The putts I hit were good ones but it was one of those days when they weren't dropping."

I was interested to hear that Mark McNulty gave Marie Laure de Lorenzi exactly that advice when the two of them combined to win the Benson and Hedges Mixed Team Trophy at the end of 1988. In his opinion, Marie Laure's only fault was one of running down her short game. He confirmed that her technique was sound and advised her to stop mentioning her short game as a weakness. "Start thinking," he told her, "that you can get the ball close, that you can make those putts."

I have positive-thinking tapes and there was a time when I would listen to them a lot. One piece of wisdom which sticks in my mind concerns how, at a hole where you have water down the right, you must not think to yourself, "Don't go right." The tapes explain how you do better to tell yourself, "I must hit left."

This advice is similar to that meted out by Tony Jacklin. He goes one step further in removing all negative thoughts where you have a 'danger' drive. Instead of studying the line of the clifftop, or whatever, Jacklin fixes his gaze on some distant spot on the horizon. You may well say, "I've been doing that for years", but have you really trained yourself to block out, entirely, what lies immediately ahead?

Another species of pressure that I have felt is that which comes with having been a U.S. and British champion. It is an annoying pressure because it sometimes seems that being a champion it can work against rather than for you.

THE PRESSURE OF EXPECTATION

For example, I will be asked to do press conferences week after week, even at moments when I have just taken a last round 79 and blown a championship.

I will comply with all these requests because I am told it is good for the tour but there are often occasions when people are not prepared to make any allowances in return. For instance, there has been the odd time when, perhaps because I have been overdoing things, I have slipped up at one of these press conferences and given a very straight answer rather than a pretty lie to some awkward question. The occasion which comes to mind is the 1988 Toshiba Players' championship at Old Thorns in Hampshire.

Old Thorns has the making of a great course but, when they asked me what I thought of the greens, a picture of the somewhat worse-for-wear surfaces at the fourth and fifteenth holes swam across my mind and the reply which escaped my lips was "Horrible!" There were plenty of good things I could have found to say about the course (there were several interesting holes; the trees were at their autumnal best; I had just shot a 69) but that day I was in no mood for beating about the bush and, upset though everyone was at my comments, there was no getting away from the fact that a couple of the greens were in no fit shape for our Players' championship.

The way of life on the professional circuit is such that you get plenty of situations where a player will come out with something which she would have done better to keep under her hat. Certainly, the following incidents, both surrounding the same girl, would have to go down as uncontrollable reaction to the intrinsic disciplines attached to playing stroke-play week after week.

The girl in question, Lori Garbacz, was heading for a good finish in one tournament when she deliberately blew it, suddenly having this burning desire to see how the packed galleries in the greenside stand would respond were she to hit a ball clean over the top of them. To the amazement of her caddie, who had recommended an eight iron, she reached for a three wood and hit a shot which was still rising as it cleared the stand.

On another occasion, she was set to wind up somewhere in the top ten after hitting a lovely little pitch to within three inches of the flag at the eighteenth.

"Is that good enough?" she called jovially as she came within earshot of the crowds surrounding the green.

"Sure," came a voice from the stand, "we'll give you that!"

"Thanks," replied Lori.

Whereupon, to the mingled astonishment and disbelief of those watching, she bent down and picked the ball up, getting herself disqualified in the process. There was no question of her having had a mental aberration. She simply wanted to see what the crowd would make of it.

That Old Thorns incident aside, the only other time I have had a slight altercation with officialdom in recent years was when I withdrew from the 1988 Variety Club Classic at Calcot Park. Having suddenly felt overcome with exhaustion midway through the Nestlé World championships in the States, I put a call through to the W.P.G.E.T. at Tytherington.

The only trouble was that my phone call, made the instant I came in off the course after my first round, was too late, because of the time-change, to catch anyone in at the European tour's headquarters. When I rang back the next day, I had gone beyond the pulling out deadline and was given an automatic fine of £75.

The money did not worry me but I felt, strongly, that there should have been a bit of give and take. The line the committee was taking was "Why should Laura get any different treatment from anyone else?" If you think about it, though, the player in my position is slightly different in that she is constantly being asked to do things the others are not.

PRESSURE FROM HITTING LONG

The pressure I put on others through hitting a relatively long ball is not what many might think. Although it is great to be a big hitter, you have many more options to consider than the player who hits an average ball. Where the latter can reach for his or her driver off every tee, someone like me almost always has to consider whether she is likely to run out of fairway if she takes a driver or whether she wouldn't do better to choke down and take a two iron.

Hitting a long drive also means that your playing partner is almost always going first for the green. It was at Old Thorns' ninth that I remember nailing a drive and finishing some ninety yards past my playing companion, the former English internationalist, Pat Smillie. In that instance, the feeling of satisfaction

I had from catching one right out of the middle was rudely interrupted as Pat, a thoroughly well-organised golfer, hit her long iron to within a few feet of the flag.

I found myself in a situation where I had a sand-wedge in my hand, together with the feeling that I could look silly if I didn't hit my shot inside hers.

Although I gather that America's Peggy Conley once said that she not only went out of her way to avoid watching me hit but tried to avoid hearing the strike; the women professionals are not like the occasional *pro-am* partner who wants nothing more than to go back to his mates and say that he struck one past me.

The professionals know that length is not everything and that I am not going to win every week. So much can depend on whose eye is in on the greens and who can keep holing the putts amid mounting pressure.

The putt I had eventually to hole to win the U.S. Open at Plainfield was three and a half feet, possibly four, and slightly downhill. I did for that putt what I always do when I have an all-important one to make. I fixed all my concentration on putting a good, firm stroke on the ball.

Relatively sound though I would seem to be under pressure, I am sure the psychiatrists would make something of a recurring dream I have had for many years. In this dream, I am in the house and standing on a table-top, and the task is to have to hit a ball out of the window.

Normally that is exactly the kind of challenge I would relish but in this context I am faced with a problem because there is a wall right behind me and, try as I might, I cannot take the club back.

To date, I have never got the ball out of that window . . .

THE WOODS

SETTING-UP

When I look at myself at the beginning of the drive sequence, I think at once of the things which have gone before that moment when I am ready to take the club away. I will have looked up several times to see where I am going and I will have visualised the precise area where I want the ball to land.

I will also have paid plenty of attention to my set-up. Setting up correctly is more important than anything else because if your alignment is awry, not even the best swing in the world will save you. Although I do not rigidly follow the same pattern every time, I usually start with the clubhead behind the ball and then bring it to the near side of the ball while I check on the alignment of my shoulders and feet.

The clubface should be square to the line of flight although personally I turn the clubhead in a fraction at the last second. The reason for this is that I have to compensate for the slightly open stance I use to get a left-to-right flight on the ball. If I opened the clubface as well, that would spell disaster.

I have a series of wristy waggles, with the final one altogether slower than those that have gone before. At that moment, all I am focusing on is the back of the ball.

In order to make this easier, I will have lined up the ball's name and number so that that is the point of the ball which the club will hit. I was once advised, and I have no idea whether it is the truth or utter nonsense, that the area the manufacturers have stamped is the optimum point on the ball for hitting purposes. Whether it is or not, it is under this happy assumption that I launch myself at my drive.

Although it is not something I think about too carefully, I usually tee the ball up so that the top of the ball is about a quarter of an inch above the clubhead. When I am going for a really big shot, I tee it a little bit higher.

34

The clubface should be square to the line of flight.

THE SWING

My swing looks compact but it is easy to detect the slight sway I have had all my golfing days. Some see it as a fault but, although I did overdo it somewhat in 1990, it feels to me that much of my power comes from that movement. I am a believer in a short swing because so little can go wrong with it. A player with a long swing is more likely to take the club back in one plane and bring it back down in another.

You can almost 'see' the power when I am at the top of the swing. I am still looking at the back of the ball and I do not feel any

35

I am a believer in the short swing because so little can go wrong with it.

I keep my head down as I hit through the ball, while my follow-through is long but controlled.

pause before the downswing. Instead I am conscious of the swing being one, complete, fluid movement.

I keep my head down as I hit through the ball, while my follow-through is long but controlled. If you are all over the place on the follow-through, your swing is unlikely to have been well-balanced.

Looking at the last picture, you will see that my left foot has slid a bit, opened out. Something has got to give when you hit the ball hard and I do not see that this does any harm.

Just as there are those who wince at my sway, so there are those who find fault with my grip, saying that my right hand is too far on top. As I see it, mine is a solid swing in which everything has worked together to contribute towards a good, long hit.

When I read an analysis by other people of my swing, I find it difficult to take in that they are talking about me. Having learned by imitation, I want nothing more than a picture of a good swing in my mind. In addition to copying the players I would see on television, I also followed much of what my brother Tony did. It is lucky that he had such a good swing because if he had been hopelessly unorthodox, and had I been under the impression that his way was the right way, I would have copied the bad habits.

NO RESTRICTIONS

I find that the driver is the easiest club of all. Quite often there will be no restrictions in terms of length and it probably does not matter if the player veers little to the right or left. Yet it is a fact that a high percentage of handicap golfers are frightened of the club and are therefore giving away twenty or even thirty yards off every tee.

Where women are concerned, the driver will probably have been discarded because of a lack of confidence. Usually with men, the reverse will have applied, with a surfeit of over-hard hitting having led to the golfer losing a ball on every other hole.

This male failing is accentuated in *pro-ams*. Time and time again I have gone out on a *pro-am* round where nothing has given the men more pleasure than to be able to say, after we have reached our respective tee shots, "Your shot, I believe!"

METAL WOODS

Although metal woods are fashionable, the debate still continues as to whether they are right for everyone. There is no question that a metal driver will afford extra length. Indeed, when they held the 1988 American Long Driving contest in the Bahamas, they were so certain that it would be won with a metal club that an extra $10,000 was to be added to the prize money if the winner used a wooden club. He did not.

I have tried a metal driver and there is no doubt that I hit farther with it. But I am also considerably less accurate.

The Maruman driver I am using today, and I cannot see my eyes wandering, has a graphite shaft and a wooden head. For me, it seems to be the perfect combination but, of course, everything depends on the individual.

Certainly, a change to what I call 'high-tech' equipment is no bad idea for those women, and I see quite a few of them, who are looking for a more 'exciting' strike.

The more you use your driver, the more friendly its face will become, so much so that there will be occasions when you may feel tempted to use it off the fairway.

THE RANGE OF WOODS

I myself carry only a three wood because my longer irons take the place of a four and five wood. The average woman golfer should consider having a wider spread of woods. Although I have a colleague, in Julie Brown, who spends her life trying to wean pupils off the higher woods and on to the irons on the grounds that they will get more accuracy and penetration, I have an open mind.

I agree that most people hit farther with an iron, but I have seen women golfers whose confidence in their five and six woods is uncanny and much too good to waste.

MY WAY

Playing over thirty-five tournaments a year, as I have been doing since 1988, helps to keep me mentally and physically fit. It is not just the golf that keeps me fit, but the endless business of hauling heavy cases about the place and driving long distances.

There are girls on both circuits who like to go jogging and on the American tour there are those who make regular use of the L.P.G.A.'s mobile gymnasium, doing weight training and attending aerobics classes.

I understand that Mark Calcavecchia, winner of the 1989 British Open, has faith in aerobic-type exercises but, as I see it, there are quite a few competitors who do aerobics just because they are the 'in thing'. That, though, is probably a little unfair though, and deep down I have a great respect for those who stick to regular training routines. It is just that they are not for me.

For a number of these fitness fanatics, the exercise will go hand in hand with a rigid attention to diet. I know of American professionals to whom it means everything that they should go out for a round equipped with the right brand of health food bars. Sherri Turner, winner of the L.P.G.A.'s 1988 Order of Merit, takes peanut butter sandwiches as well. But me? I just grab a Mars bar or whatever comes to hand.

On the course and off, I mostly eat what I please when I please, although I did cut out the cans of Coke – I was drinking at least twelve a day – after a lecture from Gary Player.

Another concession I have made – this one at the instigation of Winnie Wooldridge, whose years in top-class tennis taught her about sports diets – is to make sure I have breakfast before a competitive round. Winnie told me that I was putting myself at a real disadvantage in not having something before I played. Not so much from the pint of being strong physically, as mentally. Your concentration is the first thing to suffer when you get hungry.

From a bunker in the
British Women's Open,
1988.

If I have an afternoon starting time I would not think in terms of eating a clubhouse lunch, for that would mean sitting down in the dining room and being exposed to too many distractions. Instead, I would have a couple of sandwiches and make sure I had a Mars bar and some drinks in my bag.

FEELING GOOD

One item I always carry in my bag is a hairbrush. It comes out five or maybe six times a round and, although I can almost hear the technical experts pouring scorn on this particular notion, I can honestly claim that a good brush of the hair can often make a difference to my score.

A lot of golf is about feeling good. I would not want to be wearing a sweater which I felt was making my shoulders seem broader than they are – something which takes me back to the nightly television coverage of the U.S. Open. Whereas all the other girls were interested only in things like the position of their right elbow and the angle of their feet at the address, my sole concern was whether my shoulders looked big.

I am glad nowadays not to have to dress up in team uniforms. Some are acceptable but I must say I never felt particularly great in the maroon and navy of Surrey. To me those colours are a little dreary and they never gave me that feeling of being two up on the first tee – a feeling which you can have if you are wearing clothes in which you believe you are looking your best.

A typical moment when I will call upon Tony to unearth the hairbrush is when there has been a pile-up at some short hole. The wait will have been a real drag if it has come in the middle of a good run of figures, while my positive thoughts will have been further eroded if I have seen those ahead hitting into sand or trees. A good brush of the hair tells me that I am ready to get up and go, that I am making a fresh start. However, just in case you should get the wrong idea, I have never fallen into the same trap as did that vastly entertaining veteran, Carol Mann.

Carol loves to tell of how, at a time when she was well-placed to pocket the winner's cheque, she started thinking ahead to the prizegiving and applied her lipstick and did her hair on the eighteenth tee. She never got to stand on the winner's rostrum.

RELAXATION

In my time off, I see relaxation as being more important than anything else. My idea of relaxation is to concentrate on a frame of snooker, to go to the shops, the casino, or the races. Or maybe to take the car out for a gentle spin.

Much was made of the way in which I went off to the shops rather than the practice ground when the fourth day's play was called off in the 1987 U.S. Open. I had no pang of conscience as I drove past the long line of players at practice, for I felt that it was best for me to get away. I had been playing well all week and there was nothing worrying me about my game. As it turned out, I never hit a shot that day – unless you count the putting contest I had with my brother and cousin down the corridors of our Holiday Inn Hotel.

It could be that that break made all the difference, for the championship went on for two further days, with the fourth round followed by the most demanding of eighteen hole play-offs.

The days when I would go shopping before a round are long since past, because I discovered that these outings made me feel *too* relaxed. I like to get a little worked up, mentally, before I play and shopping does tend to take the edge off that state of mind.

I have also stood on the first tee on several occasions and wondered less about the shot I had to play than whether my latest purchase was a big mistake. The answer is to shop after a round because that way you have the whole night to get over those inevitable second thoughts.

Talk of nights calls for a mention of sleep. There are plenty of girls on tour who will have called it a day long before I have set out for the casino. This reminds me of that old Walter Hagen story concerning how, when the great man was told that his opponent in the next day's play-off had long since gone to bed, Hagen had replied, "Yes, but he won't be sleeping."

Even if I have not gone out, I am rarely in bed before twelve. Once ensconced between the sheets, I will watch television and more often than not I will wake in the morning with the television still on.

I must confess to enjoying more than the occasional visit to the casino. Doubtful pastime though it might sound, I find it a great diversion and one which can take my mind completely off everything else. When I missed the cut in Phoenix in 1989, for example, I went on my own to Las Vegas and there joined in a game of cards lasting seven hours.

I like to win but I can honestly say that I'm never heartbroken if I lose, and this explains why I have never decided to call a halt. If it did upset me, I would stop at once.

Gambling is a lot of fun, whether it is in the casino or on the golf course. If, on the course, I take a risk and it does not come off, I do not start saying to myself, "Why on earth did I do that?"

If taking risks worries a person, he should not take them. He should not have that bet and, by the same token, he should not contemplate going for that gap through the trees.

One thing you could set against this 'vice', if you see it as such, is that I rarely drink. I would never want to do anything that might put my driving licence at risk.

There are a few players who drink in the world of women's professional golf but I don't think it fits in with the professional golfer's image. What is more, that often repeated theory, usually voiced by those who drink more than is good for them, that you play better after getting smashed, is a load of nonsense.

You know by looking at a player if she's been out drinking the night before. Physically, if not financially, she would have been better off losing money at the casino!

Another place you might find me at the end of a tournament day is on the go-carts. Many people say "What if you break an ankle?", but I have never been one to fuss over myself in that way. Some may think I go over the top in taking risks but I think it is no less dangerous to be 'too precious'. I have known players who do not dare to go ten-pin bowling for fear of the effects it might have on their swing. Quite honestly, if their swings are that fragile, they are never going to be able to cope with any out-of-the-ordinary situation on the course such as might occur if their ball were to land in a web of tree roots.

Following the greyhounds is also pretty high on my list of hobbies. Dominique, the dog I share with two great friends Alex Smith and Gordon Dupre, has recently retired but she ran fifty-three races, and I saw around half of them. Waiting for her to come out of the starting blocks gave me an inkling of what my mother goes through when she watches me play golf, and it also stirred in me the same feeling of nervous apprehension that I sometimes get on a first tee.

BALANCING PRACTICE AND LEISURE

Although it might be better to spend my spare time practising, I genuinely feel long hours of practice are not nowadays my scene. Indeed, although it is a terrible admission, there are days when I will not even practise before the start of a round. I am convinced that a bucketfull of balls, hit when I am not feeling like hitting them, does not make an iota of difference to how I play that day. And my practice rounds are not always entirely productive. I have played too many where my concentration has been almost non-existent.

Unless they are laced with bets and side bets, I do not enjoy practice rounds one bit and no-one in their right mind would want to play with me in one. I tend to get fed up after the first few holes and, as long as there are a couple of players left, I will happily head for home. I did just that, after no more than eight holes, in a practice round before the British Open I won at Royal Birkdale.

PLAYING A COURSE 'BLIND'

Tim Clark, my old caddie, and Tony, my brother, know what to expect, with neither ever reading anything into the way I play on the days preceding a championship. I rather think it was Tim who once said, "Laura is no good at all until the gun goes."

Although it goes against everything in most teaching manuals, I never feel at much of a disadvantage when I am playing a course 'blind', for good caddies such as Tim and Tony can anticipate almost everything you will want to know.

Tim, for instance, had things well under control when, because of the way in which the 1987 U.S. Open had lasted two extra days, I had to play in the 1987 British Women's championship at St Mellion without having previously set eyes on the place.

I was a runner-up that week, but there was another, more recent occasion where I came out on top after having arrived at the venue, Biarritz, only the night before the start.

That time it was Tony who had gone out early and done all the homework while I was at Buckingham Palace receiving my M.B.E.

I got to the tournament venue late on the Wednesday night, only to find that my luggage, although not my golf clubs, had gone missing. I had to buy a pair of shoes and borrow a shirt, while I had to set off on my first round in the jeans I had worn for the journey. (It is actually against the rules for us to wear jeans at a tournament site but Joe Flanagan, our Executive Director, and his team, very reasonably accepted that I had no option.)

When news came that morning that the case had arrived, I nipped into the clubhouse at the first possible opportunity to slip into a pair of slacks and from there went on to return a record-breaking 65. For what it is worth, in my first round in Biarritz in 1990 I improved on that 65 by two shots.

The Queen's parting words when I received my M.B.E. were, "Carry on the good work." I do not suppose for a minute that anyone ever pointed it out to her but I did comply with that royal command, winning the tournament by a shot from Marie Laure de Lorenzi.

I would never, from choice, go into a major championship without attempting to go through all the right motions but I must concede that I seldom prepare as others prepare. For example, for my U.S. Open win many of the serious contenders had been there for five or six days before the start, but I flew over from England only on the Monday.

Part of me tells me that those who arrive too long in advance are only giving themselves more time in which to get worked up to a pitch where they cannot hope to play their best golf. And I know that I could never stomach more than a couple of days of practice. When I get to a venue I am dying for the competition to begin and I cannot stop myself from seeing the days leading up to the start as a bit of a waste of time.

I do not for a moment think there is any special virtue in the fact that I do things differently from the average woman professional. In amateur days, when I was playing for the Surrey side and for England, I would do precisely what was required of me in a team context and I do not believe there is any captain, anywhere, who would have described me as a difficult team member. Furthermore, when I was involved, as a professional, in the 1987 World Team championships in England which were cut short by the October hurricane, I was out practising for as long as anybody. In that instance I felt it important to cover myself in case I played badly. I would not have wanted anybody to say, "Her heart isn't in this, she didn't even practise." The same applied in the Solheim Cup in 1990.

Most of the time on the professional tour you do not have to fit in with other players. There are some girls who will do something because their friends and room-mates are doing it. But the ones who shine are mostly those who stick with what they know to be best for them.

COMMUNICATIONS When I do something to write home about, I ring. The amount of money I spend on phonecalls is mind-boggling and yet nothing has given me greater pleasure over the last few years than being able to telephone my mother and Uncle Mike with good golfing news. At a rough guess, this is a luxury which costs me around £3,000 per annum but these calls cannot really be measured in financial terms.

Of course, financially, things are very different to how they were in 1985 when, practically penniless, I had to borrow £1,000 from my mother in order to get started on the professional circuit. In recent years, I have had enough money coming in to afford the two cottages next door to the family home in Ottershaw and a B.M.W.

In owning up to being a little extravagant, I might as well tell the story of my accountant asking my mother if she would like to know how much I had spent in the last month.

"Heavens no!" replied my mother, hastily, for she knew only too well that his figures might keep her awake for nights.

IRON-PLAY

**THE RANGE OF
IRONS**

The irons I carry are as follows: two, three, four, five, six, seven, eight and nine, together with three wedges. There are those who say that I should follow the example of the former American Open and Amateur champion, Catherine Lacoste, and use a one-iron. Catherine, who is today the President of the W.P.G.E.T., was exceptionally strong about the wrists and made excellent use of the one-iron.

I have quite an assortment of one-irons at home and can hit the ball pretty solidly with them all. However, I am quite satisfied with my choice of a three wood and two iron and have seldom felt the need for a club in between the two. And in any case, with fourteen clubs the upper limit, something has to be left out.

Most men will carry an assortment similar to those I have in my bag. But the woman golfer seeking to find the right blend of woods and irons should ask herself whether she would not do better to have more woods and fewer irons.

The two-iron, for example, is a club which strikes me as being essentially for strong men, low handicap women golfers and youngsters who have developed strength by hitting a lot of practice shots or perhaps by playing hockey at school.

I am a great believer in teenagers experimenting with one-irons and two-irons from the beginning. If you put off the moment when they come face to face with these longer irons, they will grow up with the notion that they are difficult clubs.

THE TWO-IRON

The kind of relationship you want to develop with a two-iron is one where you feel as comfortable and confident with the club as you do with an eight-iron. I see my own two-iron as a particularly friendly implement in that, when I use it off the tee, as I did all the time in winning the Inamori Classic in 1991, I feel I am guaranteed a spot on the fairway.

48

In taking the club in lieu of a driver, I will often hit the ball directly off the turf instead of using a tee-peg. There are experts from Bobby Jones onwards who have always maintained that it is madness not to give yourself the advantage afforded by a tee-peg, but I am convinced I get a better strike by hitting the ball off the grass. Somehow there seems to me to be less resistance. It is just a feeling I have and certainly not something I could begin to explain in technical terms.

You have to hit a two-iron hard, take a divot. You cannot sweep the ball away, nor can you afford to give it anything less than a confident clout. A nervous two-iron is a non-starter.

You want to feel as comfortable with a two-iron as you do with an eight-iron.

THE SIX-IRON

The six-iron is a club with which almost every golfer is at ease. I use it for my first twenty shots at the start of a practice session, hitting some straight and others drawn or faded as the mood takes me.

You do not need to hit a six-iron hard. All that is necessary is to put an easy swing on the shot and set your sights on getting the ball as close to the flag as you would with an eight-iron. Too many golfers, men and women alike, are far too easily satisfied with this club, thinking that simply getting on the green is enough when they should, in fact, be looking for a birdie putt.

My main thought as I stand over the six-iron is one of picturing precisely, as opposed to roughly, where I want the ball to land.

If, in a round, I have hit my middle irons wide of the mark, all my instincts tell me that I should have a stint on the practice ground at the end of the day. I would not start dwelling on technicalities but would simply be looking to rediscover the right feel – something which usually takes about half an hour.

The way in which I would set about rediscovering this feel is by shortening my backswing and playing a few punch shots. Punch shots give you a good solid strike and once you are hitting them well you can gradually revert to a longer swing.

I make it a rule never to finish a practice session on a bad shot and to shrug off any bad shot or shots I might have hit midway through the stint. Even if, in practising with a nine-iron or wedge, I have had a shank, something which many see as the most disconcerting shot of all, I do not worry.

But I do have my own 'shank cure'. I move the ball to the toe of the club for the next shot. When I do this I find that my 'golfing eye' automatically ensures that I bring the club back to the right place on the downswing.

50

Simply getting on the green is not enough – look for that birdie putt.

RULES – WRITTEN AND UNWRITTEN

**COMPLEXITY OF
THE RULES**

Universities should offer the Rules of Golf as a degree course. To my mind they are incredibly obscure and sometimes unbelievably removed from common sense.

Nowadays I will call for a ruling rather than frantically leafing through the book in order to try to interpret some rule correctly. It takes time, but the stakes in the professional game are so high that you cannot afford to make a mistake.

I have been the beneficiary of some unlikely rulings. For instance, in the third round of the 1987 U.S. Open I hit a wayward second at the ninth hole which finished twenty to thirty yards left of the green and under hanging branches. If I had had to play it as it lay, I was looking at a five at best. As luck would have it, a grandstand rose between that tree and the green and, to my amazement, an official ushered me round to an inviting little dropping zone. I still had a relatively awkward shot because I was playing to an elevated part of the green but I was able to escape with a four which had my friends and family breathing audible sighs of relief.

The kind of decision which makes a mockery of the rules is when you see someone hitting into trees, only to be allowed a free drop in the clear because the ball had come to rest on a cart track. I know this is seen as the 'rub of the green', but I do feel it is against the spirit of the game.

Things have gone too far – the number of rules is probably going up even at this very moment – for there ever to be a return to a basic sheet which can be referred to in a matter of seconds. However, until such time as there is a more simple version of the Rules of Golf, I will be relying on others to interpret all but the most straightforward rules for me. This may not be very professional, but it is probably no bad thing to draw attention to an area which has become such a talking-point among the players.

If you think I am being truculent on this matter, look back to what happened to the experienced Des Smyth in the Tenerife Open at the start of 1988. Smyth finished eighth, but afterwards disqualified himself when he learned how he had applied the wrong penalty in a bunker which, because of the wet weather, had been designated a water hazard.

As far as I can remember, he lost around £4,000 in prize money and a commensurate number of Ryder Cup points: hardly the way to begin a new season.

USING THE RULES

My genuine fear of falling foul of the rules has led to a number of occasions when I have had to hang around waiting for an official to answer my call for a ruling. Such a delay can ruin both your momentum and – which can obviously be embarrassing – that of your playing partners. For example on the second morning of the 1988 U.S. Women's Open at Indianwood, my companions suggested I should call for a ruling about the sprinkler head which was liable to interfere with my shot to the green. I waited and waited but when, after seven or eight minutes, the people behind seemed to be getting restless, and there was still no sign of an official, I began to get uptight and decided to go ahead and play.

I do not know to this day whether or not I would have got relief in that particular instance, but the stroke I played left me ten feet past the hole and contributed to my starting with a bogey. It would not have been so bad if it had occurred further into the round, but it was not the kind of thing that you want to happen at that early stage.

Having called the official I should have steeled myself and waited patiently until he turned up, and reminded myself that it was hardly my fault that the whole business was taking so long.

Since the club golfer has no-one to turn to, he or she should read and re-read the rules. Not with a view to learning them off by heart, but to gain a working knowledge of where to find the various points within the rule book.

The woman golfer, in particular, should be well versed in the rules for, as Walter Hagen once observed, there are those on the distaff side of the game who use the rules to fuel an obsession to make an opponent feel uncomfortable. "Women," he observed, "know the rules and observe them far better than men. The woman who trifles with the rules, through ignorance or hope, doesn't have a chance to get away with it."

Hagen's words bring to mind the story of a third-team club game in the Midlands in which one of the visiting players quick-hooked her opening drive into the bushes.

The host player, a homely creature who had been inveigled into the proceedings more for her ability to knock up a cake than a high pitch, involved herself in the search with characteristic zest.

Eventually, her hands torn by the briars, she emerged triumphant with the missing missile.

The visitor's reaction was not quite what she had anticipated. "Thank you – but I'm afraid I'll have to claim the hole."

ETIQUETTE

In her book, *Par Golf for Women*, Louise Suggs, winner of the British championship in 1948 and the American Open in 1952, penned a list of suggestions under the heading 'Etiquette of Golf'. She pointed out that these had nothing to do with the Rules of Golf, but merely drew attention to certain standards of behaviour that would make the game more pleasant for everyone.

Under this heading she advised readers against moving, talking or standing directly behind ball or hole when a player is making a stroke. She also emphasised how important it is that those who have called players through should not continue their game until the group behind have passed and are out of range.

Those who have seen me caught up in one of my rushing fits may suggest that my on-course manners sometimes leave a bit to be desired. In self defence, I would draw attention to the fact that Sally Little is on record as having said, "The atmosphere is always good when you play with Laura." She went on to explain that where others give the impression that their primary aim is one of doing better than the person they are playing with, I always seem more concerned with playing the course.

The most unmannerly behaviour of all to me is when a player is rude to members of the gallery. If someone were to give an untimely click of a camera which caused me to mishit a shot, I would not dream of pointing out the culprit and making a scene. Far more effective, in terms of educating spectators, is the way in which Seve reacted when an amateur photographer wanted to capture him as he was tackling a long putt in the World Match-Play championship. Instead of snarling, he broke away from the putt and offered to pose for the boy then and there. The boy got his picture, the spectators gave a cheer and Seve turned his attention back to the golf.

PRO-AM ETIQUETTE

When I am playing in a *pro-am* tournament, the reactions of those male amateur partners who knock one past me off the tee is all too predictable: they wait, expectantly, for me to say something. I can usually manage an appropriately enthusiastic comment the first time but after that I tend to say nothing at all.

If, in the circumstances, they then go on to draw attention to the fact that they have outhit me, I am apt to be a little mischievous. As often as not, I will ask, with would-be innocence, if they, like me, were using a four-wood off the tee.

There was one occasion during the Sunningdale Foursomes when, after I had struck the perfect tee shot, a less than sporting male opponent, who had been worried all afternoon about who was outhitting whom, recalled the drive, making the point that I had driven out of turn. There was no penalty involved; it was merely a matter of having to hit another one after he had played. To my eternal relief, the second drive was as good if not better than the first, with the ball skipping well past his.

Playing in *pro-ams*, you sometimes, although thankfully not often, find yourself in the company of amateurs who are there for all the wrong reasons. The worst are those who come up to you on the first tee and say, "What do we need to win?"

That kind of introductory remark winds me up immediately. It is an open secret that there are a handful of amateurs on the *pro-am* circuit who will go to almost criminal lengths to come out on top. I recall an approach made to a friend of mine whose team were leading at the half-way stage of a 36-hole *pro-am* tournament. The man who made the approach came from the team lying in second place, just a shot or so off the lead – and what he offered was 'a fortnight's holiday anywhere in the world' if my friend could bring it about that her team dropped out of the reckoning.

It was not so long ago in America that one of the top women professionals found herself hitched to an unpleasant, 'win-at-all-costs' crew for whom things suddenly started to go wrong. Instead of blaming each other, for they were all playing equally badly, they rounded on the professional. "For the amount of interest you're taking you might as well go in," said their spokesman.

The professional in question is not the type to be messed around. She did not need to be told twice and within a matter of minutes had arranged to have herself transported back to the clubhouse.

I do find the average *pro-am* a lot of fun. But I must confess that I loathe going out to play in competitions with men whose handicaps are clearly fraudulent. It is irritating to make a birdie at a hole only to have it bettered by a net eagle from a twenty-two handicap man who should be playing off eight. These 'bandits' make a lot of money out of their various bets and side-bets and, when you are the professional in the middle of it all, you get a feeling of being used.

I must say that I have never had a woman *pro-am* partner who has come into this category. All the women I have played with have been there for the right reasons. What is more, it is very good for your ego to play with some of these middle-handicap ladies, because they appreciate every shot.

They do not, like so many men, make the mistake of treating a *pro-am* like a medal round. They automatically accept the un-written rule about picking up the moment you are out of a hole.

It is not too long ago that I had a gentleman in my party who, in

55

the course of the round, ran up a fifteen. What is more, he was no Herman Tissies, the German amateur who, in the Open championship at Troon in 1950, followed a series of encouraging figures with a fifteen at the notorious 'Postage Stamp' hole.

As my man holed out, I managed a feeling "Good putt".

Why had I not simply told him to pick up? That is something I have never done because it has always been impressed on us that, basically, it is the amateurs' day and without the *pro-ams* our tour would not be the success it is.

DRESS CODES

Those times when I have felt closest to speaking out have been when the amateurs have turned up to play in totally unsuitable clothes. I remember one in a tweed coat, and another in a leather jacket.

You will probably be asking what right I have to be pontificating on golfing attire. I do not suppose I will ever be allowed to forget that £50 fine which was slapped on me in what was only my second professional tournament when I wore a pair of blue trousers which, in the opinion of the Executive Director of the tour at the time, Colin Snape, were "scruffy and detrimental to the W.P.G.A.'s image".

The trousers in question were made of cotton. They were not jeans, but you could say that they looked a little like them and, to Snape, the sight of anything that hinted of jeans was like a red rag to a bull.

The sponsor, the press and most of my fellow players, including the visiting Jan Stephenson – she finished first where I came in second – sprang to my defence. They had all sensed that I was genuinely hurt, since the clothes I was wearing were virtually the only ones I had at that early point in my career.

Colin Snape was cast as something of a villain, with the ensuing disputes being reported over the next few weeks in rather greater detail than W.P.G.A.'s scores.

SLOW PLAY

One area where I can be certain of a sympathetic hearing is in my criticism of slow play. When I play with someone slow, it has the effect of making me quicker than ever. You live in fear of getting a two stroke penalty and it does nothing for your peace of mind that officials talk to everyone in the group when you are falling behind those in front. I believe they should home in on the actual culprit instead of taking what I see as the easy way out.

SPECTATORS

Although earlier I expressed my dislike of players being rude to spectators, it has to be said that some spectators are a little difficult to please. Professional golfers tend to err on the side of caution

With Tony at the Ford Classic in 1989.

with most shots – and understandably so because they are playing for a living. For better or worse, I am not like that and if I see a gap, I go for it. There are many occasions when the challenge of attempting a difficult shot means more to me than the money.

The crowd go wild if you play these difficult shots successfully but if you mess things up they are quick to criticise. I can take in my stride the wise-after-the-event remarks, but the one thing that drives me wild is 'tutting'. It is extraordinary that people cannot appreciate how infuriating it is.

I would not allow myself to snap at someone for 'tutting' any more than I would want to have words with a playing companion. However, I must admit to having more than a sneaking admiration for Catherine Bailey, the 1988 and 1989 British Senior champion, for the way in which she dealt with two sister county players – Winnie Wooldridge of tennis-playing fame and Sally Prosser, the 1987 English Intermediate champion – at a county competition which her younger friends had seen as the ideal opportunity to catch up on a bit of gossip.

It is not merely by senior standards that Catherine is a fine golfer. In 1988, for example, she was unbeaten in the singles when Surrey won the English Women's County finals, with her best result a halved point from her match with Linda Bayman, a heroine of the 1988 Curtis Cup match at Royal St George's.

Catherine has not got where she has got by frittering away her time on the golf course. As you might suspect, she became more than a little irritated with her chattering companions, with matters coming to a head as she sought a moment's silence in which to dispatch a tee shot.

Her one-liner, born of a humorous disposition allied to a feeling of total desperation, was a devastating, "Don't let my swing interrupt your conversation."

APPROACH SHOTS

The ball is at the back of the stance.

CHIPPING OVER FLAT LAND

If I have a twenty yard chip to play over flat land, with no relief in the landscape like an odd bush or bunker, I will be looking for the ball to pitch and check at around fifteen yards. I play this particular shot with the ball at the back of my stance and use a lot of clubhead speed. It is essentially a punched shot. In many ways, I see it as the equivalent of tennis's drop-shot. A drop-shot looks delicate enough but it is not a shot on which you can afford to quit. You have got to hit through if it is going to be a success.

CHIPPING DOWNHILL

If I have the same length of shot and the path to the green is downhill, I may swap my wedge for a nine iron. I will move the ball more towards the front of my stance and will hit the shot almost as I would a long putt, the only difference being that I will use my wrists a little more. I will also employ a slightly hooded clubface to give the ball a touch of top-spin.

The chip looks delicate
enough but it is not a
shot on which you can
afford to quit.

To chip over a bush or bunker I open my stance and the clubface and cut across the ball.

CHIPPING OVER AN OBSTACLE

In looking for a high shot to float over a bush, or a cavernous bunker, I open my stance and the clubface just as I would for a bunker shot and, again as I would from sand, take the club back on the outside and cut across the ball. The secret in this shot is to 'feel' the club going under the ball.

THE PITCH-AND-RUN

Until the end of 1988, I would always opt for my sand wedge for the little shots around the green. Indeed, I had never thought of playing the little pitch-and-runs so beloved by the seven times Scottish champion, Belle Robertson. However, Ian Woosnam changed all that for me when I played in a television match with him in Japan. He explained that I was having to rely too much on spin by hitting a sand wedge all the time. He recommended using a less lofted club in order to get the ball back on the ground as quickly as possible. As you would expect, Woosnam went on from there to tell me to use a putter from off the green whenever I was in two minds as to whether to putt or chip. "Duffing a putt," he pointed out, "is a difficult thing to do."

The secret in this shot is to 'feel' the club going under the ball.

COPING WITH THE WEATHER

I cannot claim to be in the same category as the late Cecil Leitch who, in winning the 1924 British Women's Open at Turnberry, apparently "revelled in her defiance" of a first-day tempest, but I must admit that I have learned to cope in bad weather.

For years, I used to see wind and rain as an excuse for packing up but one day, in a *pro-am* tournament before the now defunct Caldy Classic, in the worst possible conditions, I handed in a 70 to win the individual prize easily. My performance taught me something about myself: that I was perfectly capable of putting together an acceptable bad weather score and that it was just a matter of applying a little mental strength to the task.

It is very much easier for the professional to cope in bad weather than his or her amateur counterpart because the professional has a caddie to carry the umbrella and shield the player from the worst discomforts. For the person who is having to cope on his or her own in driving rain, it can be impossible, on a wet day, to keep the water from dripping down the golf bag.

CLOTHES AND EQUIPMENT

The only thing the amateur can do in these circumstances is to try to stay on top of the situation, keeping things as dry as possible for as long as possible. Once the grips start to get sodden and slippery, that is the beginning of the end.

Payne Stewart, who had his best season in eleven years on the tour amid the adverse weather conditions of 1989, has an excellent method for keeping the very ends of the grips from becoming saturated as they soak in the water which builds up at the bottom of a golf bag. He inserts tee pegs into the little holes at the end of the grips. This ensures that the grips will rise above the first half inch or so of the flooding.

I myself have a 'last resort' tip for when the grips are finally wet through and the supply of dry gloves has come to an end. Instead of drying your hands before a shot, let them stay wet and simply rub them together before taking hold of the club. For some reason, this wet on wet combination works better than dry on wet.

In Cecil Leitch's day, there were no waterproofs and Miss Leitch and her contemporaries would simply wear several sweaters and be prepared to get soaked to the skin. Today there is a fine range of waterproof garments but, in purchasing a top, you must ensure that you get one which is much too big rather than too small. I have heard of golfing old-timers who preferred to play in well-fitting waterproof jackets, claiming these garments made them feel their actions were under control but I could not possibly wear anything which prevented me from making a full-scale swing at the ball.

The right choice of footwear is just as important as comfortable clothes. A good quality upper should help to slow down the soaking of the feet but what matters most is that a golfer should have properly studded soles – and by this I mean metal studs as opposed to rubber. The kind of terrain you are treading on a golf course demands shoes with a good grip. The number of accidents there were among the crowd as they negotiated the sand dunes at the 1987 British Women's Open at St Mellion illustrates how important footwear can be. Beverly New's mother broke an ankle on those slippery slopes, while my own mother took a couple of tumbles.

Those who use no studs at all are doing themselves a real disservice. I know that the legendary Mickey Wright won a number of her eighty-two L.P.G.A. titles wearing tennis shoes, but she had a problem with her feet which prevented her wearing normal golf shoes. Maybe, if your swing is as well balanced as Miss Wright's, you could get away with 'sneakers', but the average golfer is always going to lose his or her grip at some point and it does not have to be much of a slip to play havoc with the shot.

It may be unreasonable, but I get quite upset when people turn up to play in a *pro-am* tournament in trainers – if they want to play well they should give themselves every possible chance.

Wearing correctly spiked shoes is not in itself enough. On a wet day, the muddy turf will wrap itself around the spikes until the spikes are rendered redundant. You should check on this build-up of mud when you walk on to the tee, for it is while playing a full-scale drive that you are most likely to slide.

Aside from scraping the soles of your shoes, you will need to work on your clubs a little, running a tee-peg along the grooves. Before you strike the ball, try to dry the face of the club, because too much water will tend to wash out spin from the shot and pave the way for the kind of 'flier' you often get from the rough. At the end of the day, you must remove the damp covers from your woods and dry all the clubs indoors, without exposing them to any artificial heat.

BAD WEATHER RULES

Jack Nicklaus has pointed out that your knowledge of rules relating to casual water will need to be as watertight as your shoes. Casual water is defined in the rules as "any temporary accumulation of water which is visible before or after the player takes his stance and is not in a water hazard. Snow and ice are either casual water or loose impediments at the option of the player. Dew is not casual water."

Rule 25 allows you to obtain relief from casual water without penalty anywhere on the course by lifting and dropping the ball on drier land. You may not drop it closer to the hole or, if you are in a hazard, outside the hazard. The other thing to remember is that you *can* clean the ball when you lift it.

POOR WEATHER EXPERTS

In Europe, the names you are most likely to find at the top of the leaderboard on a wet day are those of Corinne Dibnah, Dale Reid, Gillian Stewart and Jane Connachan. Corinne is an Australian who has what it takes to 'guts it out' on a wet day. The others I have mentioned are Scots who carry on without complaining because they have always known worse. Muriel Thomson, who retired midway through 1989, is another Scot who was in her element in bad weather. Indeed, towards the end of a long summer on the Continent, Muriel was just itching to get back to the chill and icy winds of Aberdeen.

It is interesting to look at the Scots' records, for all of them appear to find it easier to win in Britain than in hotter climates. Dale, for instance, has won seventeen of her nineteen titles at home, while of Muriel's nine wins not one was overseas.

Jan Stephenson would be my choice as the best bad weather golfer in America. Unlike so many of us, she has the necessary nerve to stand there for an extra minute and wait for the wind to drop. She is always one hundred per cent organised and her clubs would be the last to get wet.

When it comes to our Walker, Ryder, Curtis and now Solheim Cup matches against the United States, there is the perennial argument as to whether it is to our advantage for the weather to be bad. Until we started winning some of these matches, people used to think it was just wishful thinking on the part of the British press, but there is clearly more to it than that. Having played among the Americans in both the amateur and professional arenas I am certain that we are better in adverse circumstances. The Americans like to have the sun on their backs. They tend to slow down when it starts to get wet and windy, and although in itself that is no bad thing, it does suggest that they are unable to take difficult weather conditions in their stride. Nor, for that matter, can a lot of them take it when the weather gets too hot. If it is one of those days when shirts are wringing wet within the space of five or six holes, they are among the first to complain.

You could almost see the American Curtis Cup side's spirit being broken as they played in the wintry conditions at Royal St George's in 1988. Collectively, they looked frozen, even though they had equipped themselves with ear muffs and thermal underwear.

The Great Britain and Ireland players, who won thirteen points to seven, must have felt chilly themselves on the second day but they never let it show. The lead in this must have come from the captain, Diane Bailey, for she is a great believer in players holding their heads high at all times.

Diane will no doubt have a great respect for that breed of higher handicap woman golfer who refuses to allow the weather to interfere with her weekly match. West Byfleet has its share of these endlessly game ladies and even at the end of the foulest of mornings you will hear them laughing in the locker-rooms.

In many respects, they are more professional than the professionals. Plenty of those who play for pay have only to make one mistake before they start saying to themselves, "This wouldn't be happening but for the rain." And the next step from that is to say "To hell with it . . ." I know, because that is precisely how my mind used to work until that day at Caldy.

MENTAL STRENGTH

The golfer will be stronger, mentally, if he or she is well prepared, physically. And by that I mean that he or she should have a reserve supply of gloves and enough extra clothing to stay warm, even if conditions go from bad to worse. I do not suppose there is a girl golfer living who has not been through a stage of thinking there was something 'cool' about braving the elements without very much protective paraphernalia, or who vowed that she would not be seen dead in a woolly hat. Thankfully, I do not feel self-conscious in a tweed or waterproof cap, although I still feel like that about woolly hats.

I think it is fair to say that nowadays I am as well organised as most players, although my mother will tell you that it is not too long ago that I would walk down the middle of the fairway getting soaked while Tony would be under the umbrella. Gradually, and only gradually, I realised the folly of my ways.

Today, when Tony and I have to face the prospect of going out on some grim, rain-lashed morning, we will work out what we might need in the way of towels, caps and extra sweaters. Then, thinking of the round itself, we will discuss how we are bound to drop a few shots but how we will make a few birdies.

In appalling weather poor Tony has to work twice as hard as usual to keep everything under control, but his main role is to persuade me to take my time, for it is too easy to rush a shot when you are hitting in the middle of an icy squall. "Knuckle down," is the fraternal instruction which constantly rings in my ears.

TROUBLE SHOTS

BUNKER PLAY

To no small extent, the manner in which you walk into a bunker will dictate whether or not you are going to get the ball out successfully. If you walk wearily into the sand thinking "I've ruined everything", you are likely to mess things up and run up a six or a seven.

It helps if, like me, you actually *enjoy* bunker shots but even if you do not you should be thinking positively as you step into the trap. Take in the consistency of the sand and work out where the ball will need to land if you are to save your par.

Some people see the bunker shot as a lazy-looking stroke. Good players often make it look that way but the truth is that the bunker shot needs to be attacked in a positive rather than a laid-back manner.

For the 'big' bunker shot, one of twenty yards or more, I will be aiming well left of target and have my club-face open so that it is almost lying flat, looking up at the sky. I swing the club back far outside the line before cutting smartly, not violently, through the sand. Wherever possible, I follow right through because that stops me from quitting on the shot.

Where the bunker shot is around the ten yards mark, I will not face so far left. My backswing will be correspondingly shorter but I will still hit the ball reasonably hard.

I am not being more precise over what you must and must not do because I am convinced that the bunker shot is one in which nothing matters as much as 'feel'.

It is essential that you find a bunker (and I know that not every practice ground has one) where you can hit hundreds and hundreds of bunker shots. Try them from that part of the bunker where the sand is at its heaviest and try them from areas where there is only a thin spread of sand. You should not just practise from flat lies and gentle upslopes, but from lies where the ball is above and below your feet and from the bunker's back.

66

The manner in which you walk into a bunker will dictate whether or not you are going to get the ball out successfully.

The bunker shot needs to be attacked in a positive rather than a laid-back manner.

You need to be adaptable, because you are never going to find two bunkers which are exactly the same. What is more, neighbouring courses in Surrey can have bunkers as different as those you might find in countries as far apart as the U.S.A. and Japan.

My idea of a good bunker is one where the ball will 'plug' only if it lands in the face of the trap. A bad bunker is one where there is too much sand and the ball plugs almost every time.

Many people allow panic to set in if they fail to escape from a bunker at their first attempt. This is obviously a great mistake: it is the panic rather than that one bad shot which will make the difference between a good and bad round.

In my third round in the 1987 U.S. Open I took five at the short twelfth where, after hitting my tee shot to the back of the left-hand greenside bunker, I moved my second only to the front of the trap. I am sure there were people who thought that that was the beginning of the end, but I succeeded in putting the ensuing five – my only double-bogey of the week – behind me and went on to finish with a level par round of 72.

Nothing matters as
much as 'feel'.

If you have a shot to play out of the rough, make your first move one of gripping the club a little tighter. Hood the clubface a fraction to allow for the interference of the grass as you come into the ball and hit the ball harder than would be the case from the fairway.

PLAYING FROM THE ROUGH

Playing from the rough is a matter of hitting and hoping. I usually take the same club as I would from the fairway and it is only when I suspect that I am going to get a flier that I will take a couple of clubs less.

I do not know how you react after hitting a ball into the rough or trees but I do know that Nancy Lopez has got it right. Whatever happens, Nancy never stops 'thinking par'.

She plays out of the trouble and then expects to hole out with her next shot. Most of us tend to fear the worst instead of sharing Nancy's assumption that all will be well.

LEARNING FROM THE WOMEN'S TOURS

PROFESSIONAL CALM

If you look at the majority of the world's better women professionals while they are out on the course it is impossible to tell whether they are scoring badly or well. They have in common the ability not to get over-excited at a run of birdies or, at the other end of the spectrum, depressed about a run of bogeys.

There are some young players who naturally have it in them to stay in control but, for the most part, it is an advantage belonging to those who have been on the circuit for years have. The people I have in mind are Pat Bradley, Beth Daniel, Patty Sheehan and Betsy King, although it has to be said that even these great players make the occasional mental slip. Patty let a big lead escape in the 1990 U.S. Open, while Betsy showed more than a touch of nerves in her singles match with Pam Wright in the inaugural Solheim Cup at the end of 1990.

I suspect that the group of players who would benefit most from watching the women professionals are those least prepared to give us a chance: that small but no less irritating percentage of low handicap men who have an inflated idea of how good they are and who refuse to acknowledge the quality of women's golf. It can get more than a little maddening when some three-handicap man starts explaining how to hit this shot or that, because I would back myself to beat a three-handicap man any day of the week.

Their cavalier approach often goes with a hot-headed temperament and I know that they could learn a lot from studying one of the Americans named above or Europe's Marie-Laure de Lorenzi. Marie-Laure's tempo stays the same whatever the state of the game and she never loses her temper.

Lotta Neumann is another European who is seldom less than cool. I have known her since we played together in the European Junior team championships of 1983 and, in all those years, I do not think I have ever seen her do more than tap a club on the ground.

Some people used to say that Lotta, as a relatively unknown Swede, had very little pressure on her when she won the 1988 U.S. Open at Baltimore, but that, to my mind, was grossly unfair. Lotta led, or shared the lead, through every round – and that creates an enormous amount of pressure. Everyone thought she had lost her chance when she spilled four putts at the seventh in the fourth round to allow so experienced a campaigner as Patty Sheehan to draw alongside her, but she made a deliberate effort not to let Patty see she was upset and it worked.

She returned to two ahead with a birdie at the twelfth and ultimately won by a three shot margin.

When, after my U.S. Open win the year before, someone had asked of JoAnne Carner what she thought of my laid-back approach, JoAnne had replied, "Long may it last . . ."

I had better own up to the fact that I have not always been as easy-going on the course and that there were times, in my amateur days, when I came quite close to losing my temper altogether.

One occasion which springs to mind was at the English Girls' championship at Kedleston Park in 1980 when I was in the process of being hammered 8 and 7 by Janet Soulsby, a player who the late Sir Henry Cotton always maintained would one day make a real name for herself in the professional game. I was whacking my clubs on the grass and I can well remember my mother saying she was "too embarrassed to watch".

Of the British women professionals, my vote for the player with the best temperament would go to Dale Reid (and I was saying that long before she won her singles match against the celebrated Patty Sheehan in the Solheim Cup). Dale, one of the most likable of people with whom to play, has an attitude in keeping with her swing. It never varies. She is always happy, never seeing any mishap as a big deal. Any youngster with stormy tendencies would do well to follow her.

Everyone assumes that the Japanese are inscrutable and I must say that, for ninety-eight per cent of the time, Ayako Okamoto, their leading player, has a temperament which could not be improved upon. But she does have the odd, inexplicable blow-out – such as, for example, when we last played together in Japan and she was five over par after five holes. Then, in the final round of the U.S. Open at Plainfield she had four putts on the ninth green and three putts from two and a half feet on the thirteenth. My reading of the situation is that it is not a question of nerves; she simply does these strange things from time to time.

Japanese women professionals have a far greater diversity of swings than, say, the Americans, but Ayako is beautifully correct, technically. Her timing is out of this world and although she looks as if she is hardly hitting the ball at all, it always seems it goes for miles.

BIG-HITTERS ON TOUR

While statistics say that I am the longest hitter of the moment, there are several players on the L.P.G.A. tour whose length off the tee is to be admired. Tammy Green, for instance, is an up-and-coming professional whose ability to hit drive after drive bang out of the middle of the club makes her well worth watching, although it was apparently less for her drives than her good looks that she was paid appearance money to play in the 1990 Hennessy tournament in Paris.

Val Skinner is another of the longer American hitters. What is so interesting about her is that she is a left-handed person playing right-handed – something which I spotted when she was signing autographs and which is said to be a good combination because the player has the advantage of hitting against a strong left side.

If I wanted to follow a really exciting brand of golf I would set out after JoAnne Carner or Julie Inkster, two players who between them won eight U.S. Amateur championships. Without a doubt, the attacking play they both developed in match-play is still with them. It is said that if Nancy Lopez had won an automatic berth in America's Solheim Cup side, then her wild card would have gone to JoAnne.

The crowds simply love it when JoAnne is in the fray because she is patently giving her all to every shot. She was forty-eight when she played alongside Ayako Okamoto and me in the U.S. Open play-off and yet she had nothing of the 'seen it all before' approach. Every championship is an adventure to her and, win or lose, she is never less than magnificent. Pat Bradley says that when she joined the tour in the early Seventies, JoAnne's hard-hitting, 'go-for-broke' golf was the talk of the circuit. "Everything about her," remembers Pat, "was more aggressive than the rest of us – even down to the way she walked the fairways."

Julie Inkster is sometimes a little fiery, but she is capable of making five or six birdies in a row. In the 1988 Atlantic City Classic she pocketed nine birdies in her last twenty holes and ultimately won on the nineteenth hole against a dumbfounded Beth Daniel. Then, at the 1989 Dinah Shore tournament, where she led from start to finish, she had five birdies in the first eight holes of her second round. But nothing tells more about her fighting spirit than that she has finished on the winning side of all four of the play-offs in which she has been involved over the last five years. Her personal favourite is the victory in the Crestar Classic in Portsmouth, Virginia, when she came up with a nineteenth-hole eagle to topple the mighty triumvirate of Nancy Lopez, Rosie Jones and Betsy King.

The women professionals and those who watch them seem to share the view that play on the L.P.G.A. tour is getting more positive by the week. "Lay up on a tough shot or lay back on a Sunday and you'll be passed by a brigade of hard-chargers," wrote Tim Rosaforte in a recent edition of America's *Golf* magazine.

Opposite:
With the Laing Classic Trophy I won in 1989.

UNEXPECTED WINNERS

One of the most interesting things to me about the L.P.G.A. tour is the number of players who come good long after everyone has given up hope on their behalf. For instance, Kathy Postlewaite's career epitomises the wisdom of that old cliché 'If at first you don't succeed . . .'

Forty-two years of age in 1991, Kathy joined the tour in 1974 and although she had five second-place finishes, had to wait until 1983 for her first win. Having won, she faded to the point where she slipped from twentieth on the money-list in 1983 to seventy-fourth in 1984.

But still she kept at it and, by the end of the 1988 season, had two more wins to her name. That year she finished eleventh on the money-list, with her scoring average 72.16 and her season's earnings $202,685.

Kathy Whitworth, captain of the winning American Solheim Cup side, was another late-developer. Many people feared for her when she turned professional in 1958 at the age of nineteen.

She says herself that she had a poor swing and that she had failed to get any good amateur results under her belt. Her scoring average, in her first year on tour, was an horrific 80.30 and it was not much better in her second season. Yet in 1963 she was second on the money-list. Kathy went on to win a total of eighty-eight titles including three L.P.G.A. championships.

Encouraging stories though these are for other women professionals who are taking time to settle, they should also give hope to club golfers who feel they are not making any headway. The professionals improve, mentally, through years of practice, and there is no reason why the club golfer should not, in time, learn how to build a good score.

AROUND THE GREENS

Club golfers can also take heart from the way in which the professionals get better and better on and around the greens, with Kathy Whitworth, as Nancy Lopez described it so graphically, being able to get "up and down from a trash can". I often marvel at the way in which the veteran players on the tour make so much of their short games. Indeed, although I learned golf by watching players like Bernhard Langer and Seve Ballesteros on television, I can appreciate why a high percentage of golfers prefer to study the women, because it is easier for club golfers to relate to the way women play.

In the specialised area of bunker play, the best exponent in my book is Australia's Karen Lunn. Karen 'reads' the sand particularly well and it seems to make no difference to her whether the ball is lying in a furrow or half-plugged in the sand. She approaches every bunker shot with the same expectation of success. But if, as a spectator, you get involved in conversation with this friendly Australian, do not start with "I've come to see how you make out in bunkers!"

This reminds me of the tale about that former President of the L.P.G.A., Carol Mann, when she came over to Europe to play in one of the Colgate European Opens in the 1970s. When Carol had this most delicate of pitch shots to play to Sunningdale's eighteenth green, an official issued a warning through his megaphone to spectators standing to her right. "Watch out!" he cried, "Miss Mann might shank."

Although I agree with the theory that men professionals generally have the edge over the women when it comes to chipping and putting, I would have to say that Nancy Lopez, Sally Little and Jan Stephenson are virtually equal to men when it comes to putting.

Corinne Dibnah and Alison Nicholas are other good putters on the European tour. I was not surprised to learn that Alison had been a wonderfully deft tennis player before she had turned to golf on her father's advice. Dr Nicholas thought that her height – she is around the five-foot mark – might stop her from reaching the top in tennis but that it was unlikely to hold her back in the golfing arena. Small though she is, Alison times the golf ball well enough to keep within range of the longest hitters, while her judgement of distance on the greens is first class.

In any study of the British girls on the greens, I think most would arrive at the conclusion that the player whose putting does least for her is Dale Reid. Dale, who has won more tournaments than anyone on the European circuit – nineteen at the last count – does have her good times on the greens, but there are many rounds when she suddenly has a couple of three putts from nowhere. Heaven help the rest of us if she ever sorted it out!

PUTTING

Nothing matters more in putting than that it should be kept simple and positive. Where technique is concerned, common sense provides the answers.

Although every seaside putting green is peopled with contorted holidaymakers holing putts from everywhere, the fact remains that the more serious student, the one whose putting is going to have to stand up to playing in the monthly medal and beyond, will do best to have shoulders and feet lined up parallel to the intended path of the putt.

It is obvious that the grip should complement the stance in terms of helping the golfer take the head of the putter straight back and straight through. Bobby Locke, the late quadruple Open champion, stood one way and putted the other, but he was very much a 'one-off'.

The putting stroke must have a definite rhythm, with the club-head accelerating rather than decelerating at impact. This is why it is so important to precede any round of golf with a practice putting session. If you miss out on this practice, your first putt on the first green is likely to be an apprehensive, "What's going to happen to this?" affair, and this will do nothing for your confidence over the remaining seventeen holes.

PRACTICE My own approach on the practice putting green is to start off with a collection of five- to six-foot putts, all of them hit to the same hole. As I develop my confidence with those, so I move on to the longer ones, eventually working on the kind of really lengthy putts which you are looking to hit within a 'dustbin lid' rather than the hole itself.

My brother Tony says about my putting:

"I think the first few putts are more important to Laura than they are to most. She is a streak putter and, if she starts holing

Positive putting, with a
simple grip, definite
rhythm, accelerating at
impact.

putts early on, there's no stopping her.''

I am among the best in the business with the four to six footers according to Tony, but nowhere near as good as I should be with the twelve to fifteen footers. He says that the other good players he sees hole a far greater proportion of these.

He recalls an observation made by Lee Trevino concerning the way in which I move on this length of putt. When I turned up to play with the so-called Merry Mex in an exhibition game, he said that he had watched me on television and itched to hold me still.

During the course of our game together, he elaborated a little, telling me that I could cut out movement by putting more from the shoulders than the wrists.

His advice made sense and, in watching leading professionals thereafter, I made a mental note of how the best of them have economic as opposed to exaggerated actions.

COMMON FAULTS

Having confessed to my faults, I will now mention the most repeated putting mistakes I see among the higher handicap fraternity. It seems that too many of them, with no expectation of success in this area, tend to get sloppy. They will take three putts from eight feet not through nerves but simply because they are not taking enough care. Their preparation may have looked impressive enough – they will have copied the professionals in lining up – but I have often wondered if they are looking for the sake of looking, as opposed to taking in useful information.

A lot of amateurs have unwieldy putting strokes, a fault often accentuated by the fact that, after all their preparation, they have failed to line themselves up correctly and must therefore make compensations in their stroke. Where they are faced with a long putt, their backswing should be no longer than is necessary to get the distance.

ROLLING THE BALL

To get 'a good roll' on the ball is all-important. To me, the best way of achieving this is to mark the ball and set it down so that the manufacturer's stamp and number are at the precise point where I will be making contact. As I stand there with my head down, I am visualising the ball running along the correct line and seeing, in my mind's eye, the manufacturer's stamp going over and over and over. It gives me something on which to concentrate and could obviously work for you.

It has always interested me that, when you get to the professional game, the men tend to be so much better on and around the greens than the women. The men's extra strength does not really help them here but they do tend to attack their chips and putts more and thus give the hole a chance. I can only think that it is because they play courses where the greens are at once consistent and consistently good.

Visualise the ball running along the correct line and watch the manufacturer's stamp going over and over.

CONFIDENCE

Especially in Europe, the women can be playing on to fast greens one week and painfully slow ones the next, or we can find ourselves at a course where there are a couple of greens which simply are not up to standard. The effect can be very disconcerting when you are trying to develop a confident putting stroke.

At club level I see no reason why the woman cannot be the equal of the man on the putting green. If confidence is lacking, she should fix in her mind a picture of a good player setting about his or her putt. This will assist rather more than any instructional watchword.

When I am putting badly, I will maybe experiment with a few cack-handed putts, but my next step would always be to try putting like someone else. Anyone can do this, the secret being to choose a good model.

The 1988 A.G.F. Open in Biarritz coincided with a time when Sandy Lyle was at his best on the greens. Thus it was that I tried to imitate the Scot. Faithfully copying the routine which had helped him to win that year's Masters at Augusta and the Suntory World Match Play championship, I just picked a spot to hit over and made the putt with the minimum of fuss.

That particular approach ties in with the theories held by the former World Senior champion, John Panton, whose daughter, Cathy, has brought shades of her father's glorious iron play to the women's European circuit. John Panton has always advised Cathy to look at a putt from just the one angle, his view being that confusion sets in when a player studies his or her putt from all corners of a green.

In Biarritz in 1988, my impersonation of Sandy Lyle worked so well that I should perhaps have offered him a share of the prize money. Indeed, the only time 'he' let me down was one afternoon when the light went and I lost the confidence I had developed in reading the greens.

PUTTING WITH LIFE AND FEEL

Of the women putters I most admire, I would have to mention Alison Nicholas as having a style well worth the copying. At the beginning of 1990, Alison featured on the putting front in an inter-European tour survey on who does what best. Although she will look at a putt from both sides and invoke the 'plumb bobbing' method of lining up, her putting stroke is as full of life and feel as are the shots she hits from the fairway. In other words, she does not, like so many, become tight and tense in pondering the requirements of a putt.

Watch Alison from the green's apron and keep watching. She is the best I know at getting down in two from this range and it is very rare for her to leave a putt short.

When you have decided on what is best for you by way of putting preliminaries, and they should be neither too long nor too short, you must harden yourself to follow them through every time.

You must not feel you have to rush when people behind are making it all too obvious that they are desperate to play to the green. This is easier said than done. Only last year, in one of my stints in the United States, I found myself in a situation where the patience of those behind had been exhausted by one of my playing partners who had studied her five-foot putt like someone who had never set eyes on a five footer before. When I went to tackle my putt, I had the feeling that our time was up. Almost inevitably, I missed.

Another circumstance in which you could feel tempted to dive headlong into a putt is when the pressure is such that you cannot wait to get it out of the way.

Harry Bannerman, the former Ryder Cup player, had just such a putt to tie the Benson and Hedges International tournament some years ago. That he hit it far too quickly was brought home to him later that night by Tony Jacklin. Jacklin's point was that Bannerman should have stood there and taken the pressure before attempting the stroke.

Peggy Conley, I gather, did much the same in the 1989 A.G.F. Open in Biarritz. She hit her three to four footer on the last green long before she was fully composed – and ended up losing at the nineteenth to Dennise Hutton, the Australian teaching professional who made such ground over the last few weeks of the 1989 circuit.

Obviously, if you miss a putt at that stage of a tournament, you are going to kick yourself for a day or so. But if you miss one in the middle of a round, you cannot afford to dwell on it. As Jack Nicklaus has said, "Life goes on. Here's another tee, another hole, another challenge. I try to do the only thing that really makes any sense in competitive terms: erase the past from my mind to make room for the present."

CHANGING PUTTERS

If my first two tricks – putting cack-handed and putting like someone else – have failed to extract me from a poor putting spell, my next move would be to try a change of putter.

Corinne Dibnah, who was staying at my mother's home for the 1988 European Open at Kingswood (I was in the States at the time) put down one of her good rounds to a putter she had borrowed from what she called my "lockerful of putters".

I have between twenty and twenty-five putters. All of them have had their turn although some may have been abandoned after no more than a couple of rounds.

You will often have read how a switch of putter has made all the difference to a player's performance. It can, but you must adopt a sensible approach where the replacement putter is concerned, giving it a chance to see what it can do. If you go out to play with your old putter still in your bag, you will never think positively.

I have always enjoyed the story of how the late Sir Henry Cotton's wife, Toots, took matters into her own hands after her husband had putted poorly in defence of his first Open title.

Firmly under the impression that the putter he had used that week was wrong for him, Mrs Cotton, a good enough golfer to have won the Austrian Ladies' championship, took that implement out of his bag and replaced it with the one he had been using previously.

The first Cotton knew of it was when he was preparing to walk on to the first green in the following week's event in France. He swung round, murder in his heart. But, among that sea of faces surrounding the green, there was no sign of the culprit.

"Just to spite her," recalled Cotton, "I thought of putting with an iron." However, having decided that that would be 'bad form' he grabbed hold of the putter that was there and, to his amazement, promptly knocked the ball straight into the hole. As putt after putt went down, so Toots, in the gallery, gradually allowed herself to be seen.

MENTAL ATTITUDE

Putting is 99.9 per cent mental, with nothing counting for more than the expectation of success.

When, in 1988, I went for weeks without holing anything, I reckon I brought it on myself, because I was constantly moaning about the fact that I had become a bad putter. Luckily, Tony was quick to recognise the damaging effect this was having on my scoring.

"You'll go on putting badly for as long as you keep talking about it," he said.

Which is exactly what happened.

NINETEEN-NINETY: PATIENCE

MAKING IT HAPPEN

"Things happen for Laura," is something people would often say during my first five years on tour. Although I am a fervent believer in a person making his or her own luck, I would have to concede that I have mostly had my share of fortune.

It was in 1990 that my supply – at least for a time – was cut short. Things started to go wrong at the early-season Kemper Open in the States when I missed the eight-foot putt I needed for a birdie to go two ahead with two holes to play. Ultimately, I finished alongside Rosie Jones in a tie for second place behind Beth Daniel. My putting remained a problem until mid-summer. At which point my long game went wrong.

Each week I would remind myself that there was no point being impatient. In the first half of the season I worked on keeping head and body steady over my putts while, in the second, I strove to re-discover confidence in my driver.

My struggle was not made any easier by the press and public, who would draw attention to the fact that my season was not going as well as those that had gone before.

SPONSORSHIP

It did not help when Weetabix, who had supported me so faithfully, announced that they were going to end my sponsorship in April 1991.

I was sad to learn that Richard George, the managing director with whom I had had so good a relationship, felt that my performances were not in keeping with my talent. It was his view that I should be winning on a far more regular basis.

I would love to have been 'great' in Weetabix's eyes and to have lived up to their expectations, but I can only do my best and I have never done anything less.

Having gone all season without a win on either side of the Atlantic, I finally came good in the A.G.F. Open in Biarritz,

handing in an opening 63 which paved the way for a one-shot win. It was hardly an ideal victory in that, because of the incessant rain, the event had to be cut to 36 holes. But a win is a win and I had played the last three holes of the second round in the knowledge that there might be no more play.

It was at lunchtime on the Sunday that the powers-that-be finally gave up hope of another round and asked that we head for the Palace Hotel in Biarritz for the prizegiving.

I wore the smart but casual outfit the occasion demanded, completely forgetting that the photographers, who had been unable to get any on-course shots, would be taking all their pictures at the hotel.

That was how my picture appeared in *Golf Weekly* without the Weetabix sweater which the company insists its golfing clients should wear. Normally, a win would have merited a Weetabix bonus of £8,000 but, not unreasonably, Richard George explained how, in the circumstances, Weetabix were not prepared to make that payment.

I could not complain, for they had given me an unbelievable £200,000 in sponsorship over a three-year period. But I did feel that it was yet another instance of the jinx which hung over my season.

Opposite:
With the Weetabix logo on my shirt.

CHANGING FORTUNE

The first-round 63 at Biarritz has to go down as the turning point in my golfing year. Dave Regan deserved most of the credit for the sudden improvement in my play. He had watched one of my practice sessions at West Byfleet and noted how my habitual sway had become exaggerated. I cut down on the movement and at once began to hit more fairways.

Looking back, I had shown glimpses of my best form during the previous week in the Woolmark Match-Play championship in Madrid. I was devastated when, in the quarter-finals, I went out at the eighteenth hole to Alison Nicholas but, right up to the end, it had been an excellent game.

THE SOLHEIM CUP

The summit of my year, the event which made up for everything which had gone before, was the Solheim Cup at Lake Nona in November.

Ever since the match was first mooted, I had the feeling that the Europeans were in with a chance against the Americans. My theory was based on the fact that the Americans had been brought up on a diet of stroke-play whereas our players had been reared on match-play and team golf. We had played alongside each other in events like the Home Internationals, the Vagliano Trophy and the European Team championships and, in moving on to the professional tour, had continued to play and socialise together. It was difficult to see how the Americans, so set in their individual ways, would match us in terms of team spirit.

I sensed all summer that they were not getting involved in the match to the same extent that we were, but they were definitely prepared for the occasion when they arrived on Lake Nona's first tee on November 16. Kathy Whitworth, their captain, had re-iterated everything the press had said about the Americans having the stronger team but had warned that the one thing which might come between them and success was if they did not want to win badly enough.

We had a great captain, too, in Mickey Walker. She drew the best out of her players and deserved a better scoreline than our losing eleven and a half, four and a half margin.

At worst, it should have been eleven points to five, for Pam Wright was the unluckiest person alive in the way in which she halved her game with the U.S. Open champion, Betsy King. Pam had fought back brilliantly to be level playing the eighteenth hole and, after bisecting the fairway off the tee, had then knocked a glorious second on to the putting surface.

Betsy, clearly rattled, hauled her second towards Lake Nona, only for the ball to rebound off a tree on to the entrance of the green. I half expected her to follow up that stroke of luck by holing for a winning three, but the fact that she escaped with a halved match was in itself daylight robbery.

If that was the low point of the week, I have to say that shaking hands with Nancy Lopez on the seventeenth green, after Alison Nicholas and I had beaten her and Pat Bradley in the first day's fourballs, was a moment which will stay with me for ever. 'Well played!" was what she said, with her sincere and smiling manner reminding me of one of the reasons why I look up to her more than anyone else in the game.

Alison and I lost in the foursomes, but I went on to collect a personal haul of two points out of three by beating Rosie Jones in the last day's singles. I would love to have played Nancy Lopez or Beth Daniel in the singles, but it was still eminently satisfying to beat Rosie.

The closing ceremony was equally memorable, with the players in each side being given a replica of the Waterford glass Solheim Cup trophy. These replicas were only produced for this inaugural match, and so it is not difficult to imagine the extent to which they will be treasured.

Joe Flanagan did a magnificent job in helping to get the match off the ground while Ping, the sponsors, could not have set things up better. Heaven knows where women's golf would be without the support of that company; they have given the women profes-sionals a match which, as is the case with the men and the Ryder Cup, will dominate their every second year.

It has to be said that our putting was not up to the requisite standard. The Americans were better at attacking their putts, at giving the hole a chance. Never was this more obvious than over the first few holes. At a time when we were still getting the feel of the putts, they were already holing them.

EUROPEAN PUTTING

We discussed this among ourselves at Lake Nona, and again at Grand Cypress the following week when we went to watch the men playing in the World Cup. I followed Ian Woosnam and Mark Mouland in their first round and, as far as I can recall, neither left a putt short of the hole all day.

I am probably not exaggerating if I say I learned more in 1990 than I did in any other year. I did plenty wrong, but I also did a lot right, notably in the way in which I never let the fun escape my game. Only during the week of the million dollar Centel Classic in the States, when I was miles off line from every tee, did I indulge in negative thoughts.

LAUGHING OFF DISASTERS

On the first day of the Centel, I had hit the ball all over the place while Cathy Gerring, one of my playing companions, was putting together a record-breaking 63. It was deeply embarrassing but, belatedly borrowing from what I have learned over the years in Japan, I eventually found refuge in laughing off my disasters. Somehow that makes it easier for everyone.

1990 was not the perfect year for me, but has any golfer, even a Bobby Jones, a Joyce Wethered or a Jack Nicklaus, ever had one perfect season after another?

As luck would have it, I did not take too long to get a win under my belt in 1991. After five weeks of playing well on the practice ground and badly on the course, I suddenly succeeded in taking my practice game to the first tee at the Inamori Classic at Stone-Ridge, California.

With a trimming of out-of-bounds to almost every hole, I used a two-iron instead of a driver. That gives away the fact that I was not fully on song with my woods, but the manner in which I made the best of everything that was going right definitely reflected a new maturity in my game.

One behind going into the final round and three behind after opening with a three-putt green, I settled with a thirty-footer on the fourth and went on to hand in a five-under-par 67. I finished four ahead of Judy Dickinson and Lynn Connelly.

Among the calls my mother received the next day was one from the long-suffering accountant I mentioned earlier.

He proffered his congratulations before asking where I was heading for my next tournament.

"Las Vegas," replied my mother.

"Oh no!" said he.

HITTING LONG

As I stand on the tee, I do not say to myself "Head steady" or "Slowly back". I am simply itching to get at the ball and my only thought is about hitting a good shot.

It goes without saying that there are special shots I have hit which have stayed with me – such as, for example, the two consecutive drivers I knocked to within six inches of the pin at the eighth hole in the second round of the 1986 Hennessy Cognac Cup at Chantilly. Those two blows set me up for an eagle, and I followed it with another as I hit a driver and four iron onto the next par five green. As far as I can remember, the only other time I have had two eagles in one round was in my final round score of 66 in the 1989 U.S. Open at Indianwood.

I get similar ripples of satisfaction from the drives with which I carried the hill at the 385 yards eleventh hole during the U.S. Open I won at Plainfield and from the three wood I hit 230 yards from a bunker to within eight feet of the flag in the 1987 Spanish Open which Cathy Panton won at Vilamoura.

The excitement comes not just from hitting the shots but from the amused and disbelieving chuckles you get from the gallery when you catch one out of the middle of the club. It was a real thrill for me when Lee Trevino reacted that way when we played together in an exhibition series in Japan.

One of my favourite moments was when my inimitable cousin, Matthew, in exhorting a new American friend to see how far I could drive, was promptly hit in the chest by one of my more wayward shots, the injury creating a lump of 1.68 proportions.

Normally, the people I play with do not comment on how I hit the ball beyond saying "Good shot!", because any such remarks are often construed as a form of gamesmanship. For instance, I would never dream of saying to anyone "Your eye is certainly in on the greens today", for fear that he or she might start thinking about what I had said and subsequently lose that putting touch.

PAR FIVES

Sometimes, obviously, long hitting can be the decisive factor in the winning of a tournament. I think I can safely say that my winning of the 1986 Belgian Open at Royal Waterloo was purely because of what my length allowed me to do over three closing par fives, all of which were just in reach in two. In all four rounds the breakdown of my scoring for those holes was two eagles, six birdies and four pars. On the last day I had an eagle sandwiched between two birdies and I won by a shot from Maxine Burton.

One of the biggest differences between American and British golf courses lies in the par five holes. In America, they are almost always genuine par fives; in Britain and Europe the greens can usually be reached in two. I do appreciate, though, that there are plenty of middle-distance hitters who will maintain that British and European par fives are quite long enough.

In the United States, a long hole often demands two cracking woods and a wedge. Sometimes two cracking woods will do the trick, but usually this is a 'risk all' exercise.

American galleries share the British crowds' assumption that I am going to birdie every par five on the card. It puts a bit of pressure on me but, at the same time, explains the relief I feel when, after playing in America, I tee up at home on a course where I know that there are a handful of par fives playing as par fours.

DRAWBACKS OF HITTING LONG

One of the drawbacks of hitting a long ball used to be that everyone thought it was all I could do. They would take it for granted that my results owed everything to my big hitting when in fact my short game, and in particular my holing of the four to six foot putts, was probably as much of a strength.

Length can be a mixed blessing because the longer hitter is always having to wait. Where others can more often than not step on to a tee and hit, or go up to their balls at a par five and unleash their second shots without having to worry about those putting out ahead, a big hitter like myself always has to think twice. Waiting never helps, and it can be embarrassing.

Fear of seeming arrogant long ago taught me to say something along the lines, "I don't think I can get up, but I'll wait just in case the sound of the ball disturbs those ahead."

As recently as the 1989 U.S. Open I found myself in something of a dilemma over how best to tackle Indianwood's fourth hole, a dog-leg of 316 yards, where the carry to the green is a good 270 yards over a valley packed with pine trees and thick rough.

When I caught the putting surface in one of the practice rounds, I had visions of collecting four birdies over the championship. However, amid the charged atmosphere of the Open, I did not like to inflict on my playing companions the long delay which would have been necessary had we waited for the party in front to move on to the fifth tee.

Each day I stayed silent and each day I hit for the green in the knowledge that, were I to come up with a perfect shot, I might ruin someone's putt. As you will have guessed, the four birdies never materialised and I ended up one over par for the hole rather than four under.

I was not surprised when, at a press conference following the 66 which lifted me into a share of seventh place, an American golf writer asked if I regretted taking the risky route.

My hasty reply was that I had enjoyed playing the hole that way. I could not expect him to understand why I had persisted in going for the green without giving myself a fair chance.

Watching the ball at the Gothenburg Ladies Open in 1988.

THE HOLE'S REQUIREMENTS

There was a time when my aim was simply to 'nail' every tee shot down the middle but today – and this maybe owes something to the rounds I have had in the company of JoAnne Carner, a player who hits flat out only in certain circumstances – I get considerable satisfaction from marrying a particular shot to the requirements of the hole.

If the hole asks for a fade, I will automatically go as far to the right on the tee as is possible. That way the ball should always be travelling over the fairway whereas, if I were standing on the left-hand side of the tee and that fade never came about, I would be more likely to catch the rough on the left. For the same reason, when a hook is required, I will often be just inches away from stepping on the left-hand tee box.

Tommy Armour once said that if you tee your ball up thoughtlessly on all, or most, of the eighteen tees, you are liable to produce "a horrifying addition" to your score. He was right – and these words should shake aspiring golfers who can fade and draw a ball at will but do not use this skill to their best advantage.

LONG-DRIVING CONTESTS

I would not nowadays go out of my way to enter long-driving contests but they can be wonderfully entertaining. My earliest long-driving contests were informal affairs in which I would be desperately trying to hit past my brother Tony and his friends.

In an official context, the first I can recall was back in 1983 on the occasion of a *pro-am* tournament at Sutton Coldfield. I do not remember too much about it but, according to a newspaper clipping, I was the only girl among 160 entrants, which included 40 professionals and 119 amateurs. They gave me twenty yards, start and I surprised everybody by winning.

I did not have any head start when, on the eve of the 1986 Laing Classic at Stoke Poges, I took part in a long-driving contest involving Peter McEvoy, the leading English amateur international who, in 1988 in Sweden, was the top individual when Great Britain and Ireland won the Espirito Santo or 'World Cup'.

I hit 284 yards to defeat other male internationals such as Michael Lunt and Gordon Cosh, but I lost out to McEvoy by nine yards. When it came to the tournament the next day, I paid for all that hard hitting. I couldn't keep the ball on the fairway. Now, when it comes to these sideshows, I plan ahead a little more and do nothing that is likely to disturb my rhythm in the real competitions.

STRENGTH AND MAXIMUM STRIKE

Sheer strength can be invaluable when you want to hack your way out of the rough or put spin on the ball when chipping eighty yards to the pin. But strength and size are not everything, and to hit a long ball have to be linked to timing and natural ability.

People will always argue about whether a youngster is better to put the emphasis on hitting hard or on keeping the swing in the right groove. I have always thought that children should be encouraged to give it a go, for it is the people who hit hard who get the best 'strike'. At the same time, players have got to be able to recognise their 'maximum strike'. If you are lashing balls all over the place and losing them, you are hitting too hard.

Obviously no-one can ever be certain whether or not I am the longest woman hitter ever. I have heard stories of how Babe Zaharias, the former Olympic athlete who won two American Open Championships, was quoted as saying that she never needed more than an eight iron for her second shot when she played at Muirfield, while there are 'longest ever' tales which attached to players like Mickey Wright and JoAnne Carner.

Although we may not all have it in us to do what the Babe did and arrive on Gullane's first tee by vaulting over the shoulder-high railing surrounds, I think I can safely say that all long hitters are fuelled by the *thrill* of hitting a long ball. It is a "Can't wait to hit it" feeling and one which can be damagingly dulled by having a lengthy wait on the tee.

THE FEEL OF THE SWING

What I *say* I do before a tee shot and what I actually do are often a little different. I could swear that my first move is always one of lining the clubface up behind the ball before bringing the clubhead just inside the ball while I check the alignment of my feet and shoulders, but there are apparently many occasions when I miss out that first movement.

But, even if I have not aligned the clubhead as a first step, I will always start my actual swing with the clubhead correctly if briefly placed behind the ball. Vivien Saunders once persuaded me to plant my feet firmly before I hit, but it seems to me that nowadays there is a lot of adjustment and readjustment of my feet before striking, and this helps me stay 'alive'.

It is because that shuffling does not take me any closer to the ball that people tend to think that I am stretching when, at the last moment, I move the clubhead from inside the ball to behind it before proceeding to hit. If I am stretching a little, it does not feel that way to me and the slight sway, which is apparently born of this idiosyncrasy, is comfortably incorporated in my action.

'QUITTING' ON A SHOT

I honestly feel that most women golfers have it in them to hit the ball farther than they do. Indeed, to my mind, the greatest fault of the middle and higher handicap lady golfer is failing to give the ball a genuine hit.

This could have something to do with husbands constantly advising their wives to put down an old ball here and an old ball there, for I genuinely get the impression that it is less a physical than a mental problem. Whatever the reason, it is a pity, because these players I have in mind are mostly beautifully schooled in terms of set-up and takeaway, and the trouble all stems from a decelerating or collapsing on the downswing.

The best thing they could do to get over this problem is to listen to the crash of ball on clubhead engendered by a hard-hitting man. Whatever their other faults, most men have it in them to stand up and give the ball an uninhibited belt.

TAMING LONG-HITTERS

There will be cases where a player has no extra yards to uncover. In such circumstances, I would remind shorter hitters that they should never forget that they have it in them to make the longer hitter look stupid. It is no fun to 'rip one' past someone off the tee, only to find that that player, with her three or four wood, is time and time again knocking her second shot closer to the flag.

By the same token, a putter can be a deadly weapon to bring to bear against a long hitter. Nothing irritates me more than to hit two shots on to the green of a par five, only to find myself sharing the hole with someone who has made a one-putt four.

This should illustrate to club golfers that they should never be beaten before they set out just because their opponent is going to hit the ball farther off the tee.

But I do suitably cherish my ability to hit a long ball. Above all, I love the fact that, in a game which is all too often taken too seriously, it makes people laugh.

I am reminded of the Sunningdale foursomes of 1985 in which I was partnered by a fellow Curtis Cup golfer, Beverly New. The two of us were up against a couple of men professionals and it so happened that, from the same tees, I was out-hitting my man by around twenty yards.

After we had won, the press seized upon what they had heard about my having outdriven my opposite number and asked him how he felt about it.

As it turned out, he was less irritated with me than he was with his wife, reckoning it was all because of her that the subject had come to light. The good lady had always been walking ahead of us and, on each occasion that my tee shot had been the longer, her voice had reverberated round the course with the cry: "She's out-driven you again, darling!"

A GOLFING CAREER

Throughout the year, my post is peppered with letters from youngsters asking "How do you become a professional golfer?" Quite often, these letters will have come from children who seem to have had no contact with the game other than watching it on television.

From a training perspective, I feel this is the best first step they could be taking.

For the second step they should head for the local driving range – and there practise the art of making regular contact with the ball. This will help to ensure that their first outing on a golf course is a good rather than a gruelling experience.

CHOOSING A CLUB

Golf clubs are getting better and better in terms of encouraging juniors, but the day when a youngster can turn up at a Muirfield or a Royal St George's and say "I would like to become a junior member" is still a long way off. If you are a junior without parents who play, you must avoid those golf clubs which dictate that juniors under a certain age must always be accompanied by seniors. Your playing chances, in such circumstances, would be severely curtailed.

In ringing round the clubs in your area you will soon get to know where there is a genuine interest in the advancement of younger players. A phone call to the secretary of the ladies' section would also be worthwhile, because you need to establish, at the start, whether juniors are allowed to play in the women's competitions. Most clubs do allow this, but there are still some where they cannot stand the idea of juniors winning senior events.

I was tremendously lucky in West Byfleet. Although I joined at a time when I had hardly played at all, the members could not have given me more encouragement. Even today, when I leaf through some of the scrapbooks my mother has kept, I feel a glow of appreciation as I re-read letters sent by club officials and members to congratulate me on my progress. When I had my eighteenth birthday in the middle of the 1984 British Women's Open at Woburn, they sent a cheque for £100 tucked inside a greetings card.

JUNIOR EVENTS

It is while playing in club junior events – and a good club will run a lot of them in the holiday months – that the keener youngsters will get to hear about junior county events.

Counties organise various matches and tournaments, with my own favourite memory of Surrey junior golf being that day in 1982 when I defeated Sally Prosser at the first extra hole at Sunningdale to win the Surrey Junior championship.

I still have the cutting from that event, although I hardly need to be reminded of how, in an outward half of 48, I had one six-putt green. I played the home nine holes in 38 to tie with Sally on 86, and I then made a winning three down the 450 yards nineteenth hole. It was an eagle which had Gerald Micklem, the man who was at the helm of amateur golf for so long, shaking his head in disbelief.

According to the local paper, and to Joan Rothschild, a tireless official on behalf of Surrey and England, I hit a drive and nine-iron to within eight feet the hole.

After this result I was promoted to Surrey's first team and I was not long in that side before I was asked to join the various England junior squads. It was great to get that sort of recognition, and I welcomed the all-expenses-paid golfing weekends we would have at venues such as Bisham Abbey, Frilford Heath and Lillieshall. Vivien Saunders, who nowadays takes most of these training sessions at her own club at Abbotsley, was in charge and she kept us fully occupied, organising matches and medal rounds for the hours when we were not on the practice ground.

FINANCES

The financial help you get at this stage is all-important, because once you reach the point where you are good enough to play in the English Girls' championship and the British Girls' championship, you are going to be involved in considerable expense.

My mother and my Uncle Mike gave up a lot so that I could play my golf, paying for my clothes, my golf clubs, my hotel bills and the running of my car. It must have cost them more than £2,000 a year.

Luckily, there are grants for which you can apply from bodies like the Sports Council. Those living in England will soon get to hear about the English Ladies' Golf Association Trust Fund, a fund which helps promising juniors with lessons, equipment and expenses.

It is at the age of sixteen or seventeen that the aspiring girl or boy golfer will have difficult decisions to make in terms of how to prepare for the professional circuit. I took part-time jobs in the winter to subsidise summer stints on the amateur tour. There are those who will play full-time amateur golf all the year round but I believe a youngster needs to experience a nine-to-five job for a while to appreciate the golfing life fully.

I spent three winters keeping the freezers stacked in Sainsburys; one as a garage forecourt attendant; and another as a bookmaker's clerk (which I admit helped to whet my appetite for the bets I have today).

SCHOLARSHIPS AND COLLEGES

The youngster who hands in her homework as regularly as her handicap cards could try for a golf scholarship at Bath UIniversity or Stirling, the latter of which has had two Curtis Cup golfers in Shirley Huggan and Catriona Lambert. Another route to golf's upper levels is via the American University system. It is no longer the case that you can get away with murder on the academic front at these places. However good your golf, you will need a reasonable selection of O-levels and, in many cases, A-levels or Scottish Highers. You will be asked to sit an American university entrance exam, the Scholastic Aptitude Test, which in itself asks for a fair bit of studying.

If you think you measure up academically and your golfing results are impressive, it is worth writing to the golf coaches at the better American golfing universities. To find out which they are you can sound out some of the Americans who come over each year to play in major British championships. You could look through an L.P.G.A. Player Guide, and investigate for yourself which universities are turning out the successful players. Betsy King and Beth Daniel, two leading members of America's Solheim Cup side, are both products of Furman University, while Danielle Ammaccapane, the youngest player in the L.P.G.A.'s top ten for 1990, was at Arizona State University with Scotland's Pam Wright and Laurette Maritz, the South African who has been outstanding on the W.P.G.E.T. circuit. The various colleges go through good and bad patches and you will want to know that you are aiming for one on the way up, or one which enjoys a steady level of success.

GOLF CAMPS

You could maybe spend a month or so at one of those junior golf camps advertised in the back of American golf magazines like *Golf Digest* and *Golf*. Quite often, these camps will be manned by university golf coaches on vacation and, since it is the coaches who pick their college teams, it is obviously a good idea to put yourself in a situation where they can see you play. Today, you could complete roughly the same exercise under the umbrella of the Sports Scholarship Foundation. In July 1990, they took a first batch of prospective students to Florida, to be examined there by coaches from universities all over the United States.

It is expensive to go all the way to Florida, so you might prefer to write to College Prospects of America. If they decide you are a suitable candidate they will send off a portfolio of your academic and golfing achievements to their headquarters in Ohio. This, in turn, will be forwarded to golf departments at colleges throughout the States.

A scholarship does not include airfares to and from the States. Some colleges, like William and Mary in Virginia, ask you to buy your own books, while the 'pocket-money' you need not just at the university itself but when you are visiting other colleges for matches and tournaments is considerable.

SUCCESSFUL COLLEGE STUDENTS

There is no finer example of those British girls who have successfully used the American university system as a springboard to the professional tours than Pam Wright. Pam, whose father, Innes, played for Scotland and whose mother, Janette, won four Scottish championships and played four times in the Curtis Cup, spent three years at Arizona State University in Phoenix.

Ranked third as an individual on the college circuit in her last year, she finished twenty-second in what was her first L.P.G.A. tournament and she went on to become the L.P.G.A.'s 'Rookie of the Year' for 1989. She played great golf in the Solheim Cup in 1990, winning with Lotta Neumann on the second day and coming from behind to share her singles match with Betsy King.

Caroline Pierce, a runner-up in the English Women's Stroke-Play championship in 1983 and a semi-finalist in the British Women's championship the next year, is another player who thrived in the American university system, at Houston Baptist College. She led the L.P.G.A.'s Qualifying School in 1988 and, although she failed to follow up that performance with a good year on tour, by 1990 she was making an encouraging number of cuts.

Kathryn Imrie was in the middle of her four years at the University of Arizona in Phoenix when she won the amateur prize in the British Women's Open at Lindrick in 1988. She went on to represent Great Britain and Ireland in the 1990 Curtis Cup at Somerset Hills, New Jersey, and promptly afterwards turned professional. She had an eleventh place finish in only her sixth tournament and has her heart set on winning a place in the 1992 Solheim Cup.

Like Wales's Helen Wadsworth, another American university graduate to play in the 1990 Curtis Cup, Kathryn proved that it is possible to attend an American college and, at the same time, stay in touch with the golfing scene at home. There are players who dread teeing up at home after a stint in the United States because they assume everyone is expecting great things of them, but they have to play through those pressures.

Plenty of my American friends have arrived on tour from universities. Most of them loved those years and their golf advanced dramatically with the regular college championships and inter-college matches. But I can also name quite a few who hated their time at university. And I'm sure that I would have come into this second category.

When you are on the professional tour, you have no option but to travel but, in your amateur days, there is the very comfortable alternative of staying at home.

I can understand an aspiring tennis player wanting to escape to sunnier climates because it is infinitely more fun playing tennis with the sun on your back than it is in the wind and rain, and you will have a better chance of finding a practice partner.

As far as golf is concerned, though, there is not too much wrong with our climate. Certainly, you get to play in a lot of bad weather – but you are going to have to play the occasional round in bad weather wherever you go and it is no bad thing to get in some practice.

BRITISH TRAINING SCHEMES

Scotland's Belle Robertson has said that the golfing education on offer through the English Ladies' Golf Association's training schemes is probably every bit as good as you will get in American college golf. This particular sporting body does not have just one squad, but several, and it is this strength in depth which makes it the envy of all the other countries.

THE CURTIS CUP

Getting into the Curtis Cup team was the goal I set myself in amateur golf and I would say that that should be the target for any young girl aiming to turn professional.

The Great Britain and Ireland selectors gave me a place in the Curtis Cup squad in the winter of 1983-1984 and, to my amazement, I was then given a place in the team itself. I had not expected to be included for, at that time, there were others – notably two Scots in Gillian Stewart and Jane Connachan – who seemed to have better credentials.

With the match being held at Muirfield, it had seemed certain that the selectors would want a couple of local players in the side. (It caused a great deal of ill-feeling north of the Border and one story sticks in my mind of how, when it was announced on the eve of the contest that there was to be a display of Scottish country dancing, some mischief-maker asked, with feigned innocence, if there would be any Scots in the dancing team.)

LEARNING ON TOUR

Only a few years ago, it was possible in Europe to do what Suzanne Strudwick did and learn the game on the tour. Suzanne had had only the occasional game for the Staffordshire first team when she decided to turn to the professional circuit. Yet, despite that less than impressive record, she was never lost among the professionals. Ranked forty-second in 1984, in 1987 she moved into the top twenty and in 1989 collected her first title, the French Open. Diane Barnard is another in that category. She was an occasional member of the Lancashire county side when she switched to the professional ranks, and made no more than £376 in 1984, her first year on tour.

In 1988 she was still lingering in fifty-first place on the money-list, but she worked sufficiently hard over the next couple of years to get within a whisker of making Europe's Solheim Cup side. Dale Reid took her place at the last moment, but she still had a commendable season, winning her first title and finishing in the top ten on the money-list.

I doubt if anyone could emulate this kind of progress today. Although the European tour is still some way removed from its American counterpart in terms of overall standard, the competition is fierce enough to demand great competence in the newcomer.

TURNING PROFESSIONAL

Having turned professional, a youngster has to avoid many pitfalls. She would not want to do what I did in courting trouble by wearing the wrong things – the 'scruffy' trousers for which I was fined £50 in only my second professional tournament. Instead, she should keep everyone happy by leaving her jeans at home and going to the mandatory cocktail parties and players' meetings. It is an open secret that the girls often dread the parties which go hand in hand with the *pro-am* tournaments but, as I have discovered, you get out of these things exactly what you put into them and, if you go along intending to enjoy yourself, you will often not be disappointed. As a golf professional, you will be in danger of becoming painfully one-track minded, having nothing to say about anything other than your golf and the golf of those around you.

Playing and mixing socially with those for whom the game is a hobby can be an uplifting experience, and one which stops you from taking yourself too seriously. Whether your *pro-am* partners are in business or another realm of sport, you can learn a lot from them.

I was once partnered with Ian Botham on a day when, almost inevitably, there was a lot of talk as to who hit farther off the tee. Tim Clark, my caddie at the time, loyally made out that I had the edge but Ian was up to fifteen yards past me – at least on those occasions when he was not clearing the out-of-bounds fence.

Nigel Mansell was also a little wild, but his short game had all the hallmarks of the attention to detail you would expect from a racing driver.

Like Ian Botham, he was a fascinating partner, while nothing tickled me more than that the first bouquet to arrive at the house after my U.S. Open win should bear his signature.

At the start of 1989, I had the utmost fun playing with the septuagenarian American singer, Dinah Shore, in the *pro-am* prior to the Nabisco Dinah-Shore championship at Mission Hills. The course we played had been named after her and, as I was soon to discover, she knew every borrow on every green. It was because of her putting that we made off that day with the second prize.

I have made some great friends in *pro-ams* – and many more in the company days I have done for major sponsors such as Volvo and Weetabix.

SPONSORSHIP

The newcomer does not want to jump at the first chance of sponsorship which might come her way. I borrowed money from my mother at the beginning of my professional career – £1,000 to be precise. I have been lucky with Volvo and Weetabix, my main sponsors over the last few years, in that both appear to know as much about the game of golf as they do about their own products. Though I am now with Maruman, I will be eternally grateful for the way in which Weetabix have looked after me for so long. And I have always appreciated that Volvo do not expect my golfing career to run as smoothly as one of their vehicles.

This is important, for I know of players whose sponsors are forever breathing down their necks. There are players who have been told that if they fail to deliver the goods over the next few months, there will be no further money forthcoming.

Any new arrival who is lucky enough to have a sound sponsor on whom to lean must appreciate that, away from the financial side of things, she has to be able to stand on her own two feet. She should never rely on sister-competitors to do things for her, because it can be very embarrassing if you are indebted to someone you are seeing every day on the circuit.

CADDIES

There is one person to whom you should be able to look for support. Your caddie.

I was never able to afford a caddie as an amateur but I realised the moment I joined the tour that to do without a professional caddie would be a false economy.

There are certain rules which must apply if the relationship is to be worthwhile. You must explain how you like to play at the very outset of the union. That will be the only time when you can say, without risk of giving offence, that you prefer not to talk as you walk down the fairways or that you are happy to choose your own clubs or whatever.

You should stick with one caddie rather than chop and change, so that he or she can get to know your game inside out and you can develop real confidence in what he or she has to say.

I have been lucky in having first Tim Clark and then my brother, Tony, shouldering my bag, while my endlessly cheerful cousin Matthew Adams is always there on those occasions when Tony has a well-deserved break. For instance, when Tony took time off midway through the 1989 season to find a flat for himself, Matthew worked for me on the American tour and was at my side when I won at the Lady Keystone Open at Hershey.

A conscientious caddie can save you a couple of shots a day, but to me the main advantage is that you have someone who is so obviously on your side. The middle of the fairway can be a surprisingly lonely place when there are crowds behind the ropes and you are coming down the home stretch.

EMOTIONAL UPS AND DOWNS

Alison Nicholas, who made so impressive a start on the American circuit at the beginning of 1990, once echoed my feelings precisely when she said that you feel closer to those at home when you are away. The new professional – and the older one, for that matter – needs the support of her family and it will help if parents understand that the nature of the game is such that their offspring will suffer emotional ups and downs such as she has never had before. Telephone calls home should be encouraged and it can make the world of difference if parents can put in an appearance from time to time.

If a novice has a disappointing start on the tour, she should not make the mistake – and I have seen it made a lot in my five years on the circuit – of ripping her swing to pieces. It is worth citing the case of Trish Johnson who won the Woolmark Order of Merit in 1990. Trish became ultra-technical when she first went to America and spent several desperate months making one adjustment after another to her swing. Her boyfriend, Kenny Struckman, put her back on the right lines when he asked what it was that had made her good in her amateur days.

When she told him that it was her chipping and putting, he recommended that she should concentrate on getting her short-game back to where it was and that she should return to giving her long shots a hard and carefree hit. She did precisely that, putting all technical thoughts on one side until the off-season.

Down the years, a lot has been written on Nick Faldo and of the full-scale changes he made to his swing under the eye of David Leadbetter out in Florida but Faldo, to my mind, is the exception and most others would do better to stay with the swing that they have got.

What about the money on offer in the professional arena? **REWARDS**

The money is good and getting better and by my reckoning the top thirty players on the European women's money-list can now make a comfortable living. Trish Johnson, for instance, made £83,000 for winning the 1990 Order of Merit and a further £12,000 by way of a bonus from Woolmark. The player in thirtieth position, Alicia Dibos of Peru, made a useful £15,926. The money is far greater on the American tour, but it does not make sense for a player to head for that circuit until she has proved herself in Europe.

Almost as many as the letters I get asking me about professional golf as a career are those asking me how long I plan to stay on the tour.

I would like one day to lead the L.P.G.A.'s money-list but, to do that, I reckon I need a couple more years of experience on the American circuit. At the moment, I have good and bad weeks out there, while to have any chance of coming out on top, I would need to be in contention all the time and play there week after week instead of dividing my time between Europe and America.

I do not complicate things by looking too far ahead, but I know that the day will come when I will want to cut back on the competitive golf and have a family. Nancy Lopez – and there is no-one I admire more on the circuit – has combined golf and child-raising to telling effect, with the two activities seemingly complementing each other. Her golf continues to be outstanding and her children are as enviably natural and good-humoured as she is herself.

There is another point to have coloured my thinking in this respect – as those closest to me know – that I have always enjoyed such a tremendous family life myself.

THE BROTHER'S VIEW

Since my brother caddies for me and his influence is everywhere apparent in how I tackle a tournament round, I thought it only fair that he should make a contribution to the book. He understands my golf and, still more important, he understands me.

I have always been in awe of Laura the golfer. It is something which dates back to the earliest days when we would knock balls about on the practice ground at West Byfleet.

When we first started, I would hit the ball just past her. That did not last for long. I did not feel angry when she started hitting her drives past mine, nor, on the other hand, did I manage a laugh. It was just the way it was.

Today we work as a team. There have never been any noisy exchanges as I carry her bag, although we did have words during the 1988 Players' championship at Old Thorns. Laura complained about the condition of the greens: it was a bad week, but our on-course altercation was over in a matter of seconds and was something I put down to the fact that she was tired and fraught from having played too much.

Laura 'sees' a shot in her head as we walk up to the ball and it is only when she has explained what she has in mind do we discuss club selection. As a rule, she will make the first suggestion and it is only if I disagree quite strongly that I will try to change her mind.

If she is going to err, it is usually by not taking enough club but, in a pressurized situation, she always prefers to hit flat-out rather than manufacture a kind of three-quarter shot.

Laura is not – at least to my mind – the putter she should be. I have great confidence in her on the shorter putts, but she does not seem to hole her share of the longer ones. Lee Trevino echoed my own feelings when, in commenting on how much she moved on the middle-distance putts, he said he had been itching to hold her still.

On the mental side, Laura's main problem is one of losing interest when she is not in contention. Her mind starts to drift and there are occasions when she has subsided to a forty-fifth or fiftieth place finish when she should have been no worse placed than thirtieth.

As for her 'rushing', that starts when she is annoyed with herself. I say nothing – for the simple reason that anything I might say would cause friction. Often I will be itching to whisper "Calm down", but I have learned to hold my words and let her play through these 'rushing' periods.

I will never forget a tournament in Sweden where she was three under par mounting the last tee but ended up turning an almost certain 69 into a 75.

She had hit her second shot, with a two-iron, under a rock and for some reason deemed it playable. As I looked on in horror, she had five hurried stabs at the ball before changing her mind and

My brother caddies for me and his influence is everywhere. He understands my golf and he understands me.

taking the penalty shot and dropping the ball safely.

Maybe I should have said something at the start, but it is very difficult for me to insist that a ball is unplayable because Laura has pulled off so many 'impossible' shots over the years. Well over fifty per cent of the shots she plays which I think are too risky, are successful.

I am often asked if I can tell on any given day whether Laura is going to play well or badly. I cannot. There have been times when I have thought that the circumstances are all wrong and yet she has gone out and played magnificently. To cite just one such occasion, there was a first round in Biarritz in 1988 when she had missed out not just on a practice round but on hitting shots before she played. Her score that day was a record-breaking 65.

Laura is remarkably easy-going compared to others, taking her golf and her success easily. She does not want to talk about a round after she has played, although on those occasions when, for instance, she has hit a couple of hooks over the last few holes, she might announce that she will be flighting the ball from left to right in her next round. That would be all and she would run a mile if anyone attempted to bring her into a technical discussion.

People assume she must be more technically-minded than she makes out but that is simply not the case. If she is wanting to hit a hook, she does not have in her mind a list of points to which she must adhere if she is to make the ball fly from right to left. She sees a picture of the shot she wants and shapes up for it instinctively.

She likes to keep things as simple as possible. So much so that she finds it irritating that others should be technically inclined. If anyone asks her for a spot of advice she has a stock reply: "Go down the shaft a little."

That is Laura's cure for all golfing ills and, although people laugh, I have seen it work for some.

For all this apparent lack of depth where the theory of the game is concerned, she is very much more 'clued up' than many might think. JoAnne Carner, who has said that she sees something of herself in Laura, points out that Laura plays her practice rounds at a speed which suggests she has something better to do. That is how it appears, and I would go along with JoAnne's cheerful assertion that, if Laura were to play a practice round on her own, she would be back in the clubhouse in a couple of hours.

But I have to say that, when it comes to a tournament, I am consistently amazed at the information Laura will have up her sleeve even after the most seemingly desultory of practice rounds. If she has hit left off the tee at a certain hole, she will regale me with information as to the problems we are about to encounter.

This awareness is reflected in her off-course life. She only needs to go to a place once to know the precise route a year later. If you travel around America with her, it is almost like having a guide. She may only have been to a city once before but she will remember the best restaurants and where they are, not to mention the precise location of the dog track! All of which probably explains why, when Laura is around, I never bother to take in any of these things.

Laura plays her best when she is under pressure. On a big day – such as the play-off day for the 1987 U.S. Open – she will be quieter than usual before going out but there will be no other apparent change. I detected real nerves as she prepared to play her tee shot at the eighteenth on that day at Plainfield, but the occasions when she is nervous are genuinely few and far between. She is exceptionally positive under extreme pressure.

It was fascinating for me when, with Laura away, I caddied one week for an Australian, Mardi Lunn. Mardi is a delightful girl and a highly promising professional but, no doubt because she was not my sister, I found the experience very different.

Mardi was far more serious than Laura, while she wanted a lot more information about things like the distances of the various bunkers from the tee. Laura does not go in for such detail. She wants to know the length she must hit to the green, and only if a bunker is directly in front of a green will she ask about it. Normally, a quick glance will tell her whether or not she can clear a sand-trap or a water-hazard.

Ninety-five per cent of the time, she will practise before a round. If she is not in the mood to practise, there is no point in dragging her out. I used to get irritated but, largely because of that occasion in Biarritz, I nowadays accept that she knows what is best for her on any given day. She loves her golf and it would be madness to do anything that might detract from the fresh approach she brings to bear.

I enjoy what I am doing too. I love seeing her play and seeing how much fun others get from watching her. The Japanese, for example, admire her for being blonde, for smiling and for playing an entirely different game to that of their own people.

They go crazy when she connects with one of her massive tee shots and, although I do not exactly go crazy with them, I get a real thrill from the effect she has on them all.

At Indianwood, on a last day of the 1989 American Women's Open when Laura was at one stage six under par, every other comment to be heard in the gallery was about what club she had hit where.

How many other golfers create that kind of excitement?

LAURA DAVIES – TOURNAMENT RECORD

1981   Finalist Surrey Girls' championship
Semi-finalist English Girls' championship
English Girls' international

1982   Quarter-finalist British Match-Play championship
Surrey Girl champion

1983   South-Eastern champion
Runner-up English Under 23 championship
English Intermediate champion
Played for England in Junior European Team championships
English International
Third in Welsh Open Stroke-Play championship

1984   Curtis Cup
South-Eastern champion
Semi-final English championship
Played for England in Junior European team championships
Runner-up Avia Watches Foursomes (with Miss S. Duhig)
Third in English Stroke-Play championship
Fourth in British Stroke-Play championship
English International
Welsh Open Stroke-Play champion

1985   Turned professional
Belgian Ladies' Open
Ranked 1 on European women's money-list with £21,736

1986   McEwan's Wirral Classic
British Women's Open
Greater Manchester Open
Spanish Open
Ranked 1 on European women's money-list with £37,500

1987   Italian Ladies' Open
U.S. Women's Open
Ranked 2 on European women's money-list with £47,151

1988   Italian Ladies' Open
Biarritz Ladies' Open
Circle K.L.P.G.A. Tucson Open
Jamie Farr L.P.G.A. Toledo Classic
Itoki Classic (Japan)
Ranked 8 on European women's money-list with £41,871
Ranked 15 on L.P.G.A. money-list with $160,382

1989   Laing Classic
Lady Keystone L.P.G.A. Open
Ranked 19 on European women's money-list with £21,608
Ranked 13 on L.P.G.A. money-list with $181,574

1990   A.G.F. Open – Biarritz
Ranked 13 on European women's money-list with £36,697
Ranked 64 on L.P.G.A. money-list with $64,863.
Won 2 points out of 3 in inaugural Solheim Cup match